Radical

Radical

PRAYING & PREACHING

LEONARD RAVENHILL
E. M. BOUNDS & GLENN CONJURSKE

Compiled by David Ravenhill

Offspring

Offspring Publishers

Visit Offspring Publishers at
www.offspringpublishers.com

Library of Congress Catalog Card Number: 2016917883
ISBN: 978-0-9981096-1-9

Cover concept: David Ravenhill & Milk-and-Honey Book
Design. Interior by Milk-and-Honey Book Design.

Published by Offspring Publishers
Siloam Springs, Arkansas

Printed in the United States of America
20 19 18 17 16 / 10 9 8 7 6 5 4 3 2 1

Rad-i-cal: of or relating to the origin and root. New and different from what is traditional or ordinary. Of change or action, relating to or affecting the fundamental nature of something; far-reaching or thorough.

A certain preacher, whose sermons converted many souls, received a revelation from God that it was not his sermons or works, by all means, but the prayers of an illiterate lay brother who sat on the pulpit steps pleading for the success of the sermon. It may be, in the all-revealing day, so with us. We may believe after labouring long and wearily, that all honor belongs to another builder whose prayers were gold, silver, precious stones, while our sermonizings, being apart from prayer, are but hay and stubble.

—Charles Haddon Spurgeon

Contents

Prayer affects three different spheres of existence:

the divine,
the angelic,
and the human.

It puts God to work, it puts angels to work,
and it puts men to work. It lays its hands upon
God, angels, and men. What a wonderful reach
there is in prayer!

—*E. M. Bounds*

Foreword

The ratio of preachers *who do not pray* far exceeds the ratio of preachers who pray.

Preaching that brings about God-given results has to begin in the closet, alone with God. There is a vast difference between a *sermon* and a *message*. A sermon may be crafted well, with great illustrations and a perfect outline, but it will only reach the head — while a genuine message birthed by the Spirit of God will reach the heart and affect lasting change in the people listening.

When Jesus, after spending the night on the mountain, descended to appoint His twelve disciples, He first told them that they were to spend time with Him before He commissioned them to go and preach. (Mark 3:14) I well recall the day a good friend looked at me after bringing this verse to my attention. He said, "David, we have no right to go out and preach unless we have first spent time with Him." There is no question that this is the missing key in so many pulpits across our nation. Jesus promised us that if we go into our closet and shut the door and pray we would be rewarded openly. The evidence of this is clearly seen when you hear a message that was first birthed by prayer.

This book brings together the two most essential priorities of those in spiritual leadership: praying and preaching. Shortly after the early Church began to flourish, the disciples were forced to make a decision between preparing meals for needy bodies or preparing teaching for hungry souls. They agreed to give themselves to the ministry of the Word and prayer while appointing others to maintain the soup kitchen. Notice once again these two priorities: praying and ministering the Word. The prophet Elijah, prior to standing before King Ahab, stood in the presence of the *King of Kings*. Little wonder then that he was able to shut up the heavens, destroy all the prophets of Baal, and then later release the much-needed rain.

Our land is also desperate for a spiritual downpour. For too long we have been experiencing spiritual drought. Our churches are full, but our spirits are dry. God's word exhorts us to, "Ask of Me rain in the time of the latter rain." Asking requires prayer—and desperate prayer at that! We too need to stand before the presence of Almighty God, like Elijah, before we can effectively confront the gods of *carnality and compromise* that grip so many of God's people today.

God has not changed, nor has His power been abated. He still waits to hear men ASK; then, and only then, will He answer and transform our *sermons* into *messages* and our churches into centers of revival and evangelism.

David Ravenhill, 2016

Get Unctionized!

The tragedy of the hour is that we have too many dead men giving out dead sermons to dead people. Why? Because the strange thing today which exists in the pulpit is a horrible thing: it is preaching without unction.

What is *unction*? It's hard to define. Preaching without unction kills instead of giving life. The unctionless preacher is a savor of death unto death. The Word does not live unless divine unction is upon the preacher. Preachers, with all thy getting—get unction from above!

Preaching is a spiritual business. A sermon born in the head reaches the head, but a sermon born in the heart reaches the heart. Unction cannot be learned, but only experienced through prayer. Unction is like dynamite—it will pierce, it will sweeten, it will soften. When the hammer of logic and the fire of human zeal fail to open the stony heart, unction will succeed.

Away with this powerless preaching, which is unmoving because it was born in a tomb instead of a womb, and nourished in a fireless, prayerless soul. If God has called us preachers to the ministry, then we should get *unctionized*. With all thy getting—get unction, lest barrenness will be the badge of our unctionless intellectualism.

Prayerfully yours, Leonard Ravenhill

Preaching

GLENN CONJURSKE

From the Author

When I began to write this book, I intended to write only a few pages for the perusal of a friend. But my heart was full, and I knew not how to stop. And indeed, my whole heart has gone into this little book. Here are the meditations of fifteen years, written with many tears. May the unction of the Holy Ghost rest upon these pages, and upon the heart and mind of the reader.

Glenn Conjurske
September 20, 1983

Good Preaching:

WHAT IT IS & WHAT IT ISN'T

Copiously illustrated from Scripture and History
GLENN CONJURSKE

I believe that good preaching is a very rare thing in our day. The shallow, lukewarm, and worldly state which generally pervades the church is not very likely to produce good preachers. And the sort of preaching which is generally heard today is not very likely to do much to remedy the low state of the church.

So the church sinks deeper and deeper into worldliness and "lukewarmness" — *while the world goes to hell.*

How solemn a matter it is to preach the Word of God in such a day! How earnestly ought every preacher to inquire, *"What constitutes good preaching?"* and *"How does my preaching compare with the standard?"*

Now it must be evident that good preaching is that which accomplishes its end. It is that which does solid and permanent good to the souls of men. It is that which draws, awakens, convicts, converts, sanctifies, edifies, and sets to work. But what sort of preaching will do this?

To put the matter simply, it is the preaching of the Word of God in the power of the Holy Ghost. But human nature being what it is, every preacher is likely to think that that is a description of his own preaching, even though few are drawn by it, and few or none awakened, converted, or thrust forth into the harvest field.

What then constitutes *Good Preaching*? We may consider this as to the *matter of it*, the *manner of it*, and the *effects of it*.

The Matter of Good Preaching

The *matter*, of course, must be the Word of God. But there is room here for great deception. Every sort of error under the sun claims the Bible for its support. But beyond that, there are many who indeed take the matter of their preaching from the Bible, whose preaching is yet likely to accomplish very little good. For they are occupied primarily with speculative points of theology, or prophecy, or typology, to the neglect of "the weightier matters of the law."

Moreover, men may preach the letter of Scripture, and be altogether wanting in the spirit and power of it. There are many preachers who are much devoted to preaching and teaching on prophecy. Yet their message bears little resemblance to the message of the prophets. The message of the prophets is primarily a *moral* one, not an *intellectual* one. Their writings are full of searching rebukes, of powerful persuasion, of gifted reasoning, of tender pleading. But all of this is ignored by the modern preachers of prophecy, and they are occupied entirely with the charting of the course of future events.

How often have I, with grief, observed (in seeing an announcement of special meetings at some church) that they are to have another "prophetic conference." My whole soul cries out: *the last thing in the world they need!*

They are up to their ears already in prophecy and dispensationalism, and yet, for all of that, are materialistic and worldly; they do not win souls, are not fervent in prayer, and do not thirst for revival. They may have the letter of Scripture, but they do not have the spirit and power of it.

They have been long fed upon a diet which is designed primarily to instruct the intellect, and they have been put to sleep by it. They stand in desperate need of that preaching which will convict the conscience and stir the heart.

The spirit of God has come to convict the world of sin, and of righteousness, and of judgment. And these three things ought to occupy a large part of our preaching to the world.

Observe, he is not come to *instruct the world*, but to *convict it*. I have nothing to say against instructing men, but I do say it is not the first thing they need. All men have a certain amount of light, but they do not obey the light which they have. They do not do as they *know* they ought. They need to be moved, awakened, persuaded. They need to be made to *feel what they know*. They need to be convicted.

They need to be convicted of these three elementary things: sin, and righteousness, and judgment.

The Bible is a book very largely about these three things. Whether we look at the historical books of the Old Testament, the Proverbs, the Prophets, the Gospels, the Epistles, or the Revelation, the great burden of the message everywhere is sin, and righteousness, and judgment. How is it that so many preachers can preach from the Bible, week after week, and say so little about these three things?

Sin, and righteousness, and judgment; let us look at each of them briefly, and so learn what must be the *matter* of that preaching which is in line with the testimony of the Holy Ghost.

Sin

Good preaching ought to aim at producing conviction of sin, as the first and foremost thing. The one great need of the world today is conviction of sin. And how little of it do we see! How seldom do we see sinners weeping and mourning for their sins. How seldom do we see them trembling and astonished, falling down and crying out, "What must I do to be saved?"

How many preachers have preached for many years and never once beheld such a sight? The times have been when such things were seen every day in the church of God, but alas, such times are no more. Conviction of sin seems to be a thing of the past. And what wonder, since so little of the present-day preaching even aims at producing it?

The energies of the preachers are dissipated in refuting evolution, in fighting profanity on television, in trying to fit the events of the Middle East into the calendar of prophecy, and even in many things more necessary and profitable than these, and yet to the neglect of the one thing needful, to wit, to bring the conscience of the guilty rebel face-to-face with thrice-holy, sin-avenging God.

We refute the errors of the cultists, and yet the cultist are not saved. Let them but be convicted of sin, and their errors will evaporate.

We preach "apologetics," refute evolution, prove the existence of God, and yet infidels and skeptics remain just where they were. But let them once be convicted of sin, and their infidelity will fly out the window.

We aim at the wrong thing in dealing with sinners, and therefore we get nothing. Charles G. Finney, speaking from a lifetime of experience as a powerful evangelist, says, "Universalism, Unitarianism, and indeed all forms of fundamental error, have given way and fallen out of sight in the presence of great revivals. I have learned, again and again, that a man needs only to be thoroughly convicted of sin by the Holy Ghost to give up at once and forever, and gladly give up, Universalism and Unitarianism."[1]

Finney elsewhere relates the following: "The case of an infidel of my acquaintance may serve to illustrate this. He had lived in succession with two pious wives; had read almost every book then extant on the inspiration of the Scriptures—had disputed, and caviled, and often thought himself to have triumphed over believers in the Bible, and in fact he was the most subtle infidel I ever saw.

"But at length a change came over him, and his eyes were opened to see the horrible enormity of his guilt. I saw him one day so borne down with sin and shame that he could not look up. He bowed his head upon his knees, covered his face, and groaned in agony. In this state I left him and went to the prayer meeting.

"Ere long he came into the meeting as he never came before. As he left the meeting he said to his wife, 'You have long known me as a strong-hearted infidel; but my infidelity is all gone. I can not tell you what has become of it—it all seems to me as the merest nonsense; I can not conceive how I could ever have believed and defended it.'"[2]

He also relates the case of a Universalist who actually came to the meeting armed with a pistol to shoot him for converting his wife from Universalism. He says, "He listened awhile, and then all at once, in the midst of the meeting, he fell back on his seat and cried out, 'O, I am sinking into hell! O, God, have mercy on me!' Away went his Universalism in a twinkling; he sees his sin, and now he is sinking into hell."[3] I could relate other incidents of the like nature, but I forbear.

It is evident that the preaching which does the task is the preaching which convicts of sin. Now to produce this, we must at any rate aim at it. We must give sin a large place in our preaching, even as it has a large place in the Bible.

Neither must we be content to preach against sin in general, for to that all the world will say, *"Amen"* — and apply the whole *to their neighbors.*

We must preach closely, searchingly, and specifically, warning the sinner not only against sin in general, but against "his wicked way" (Ezek. 33:8-11) — against "all his sins that he hath committed." (Ezek. 18:21) We must make sinners to understand and feel that their way is wicked, that their sins are an offense and abomination to God. We must beat them out of every hiding place, strip them of every excuse, and bring them to stand with their mouths stopped, self-condemned, guilty before God.

This is the first great end of preaching.

Righteousness

Good preaching will make men hunger and thirst after righteousness. It will persuade them that there is no happiness and no salvation without it. Righteousness is *rightness*. It is being and doing right. It is to "Cease to do evil" and "Learn to do well." (Is, 1:16-17) It is to repent, and bring forth fruits appropriate for repentance.

This was the message of Christ and all of his apostles. Christ commanded that "repentance and remission of sins should be preached in his name among all nations." (Luke 24:47) The great burden of the apostle Paul's preaching (so he tells us), from the beginning to the end of his career, was "that they should repent and turn to God and do works meet for repentance." (Acts 26:20)

Yet for all of this, there is a great antipathy in the church today against the preaching of repentance and works suitable for repentance.

Many, on the plea of upholding the doctrine of *salvation by faith*, deny altogether the necessity of repentance. Others so define it as to explain it away. There is a general feeling everywhere, expressed or unexpressed, that a man may be saved without being righteous. By this means men think to uphold the doctrine of salvation by grace.

But the Bible is everywhere explicitly against them. "Know ye not that the unrighteous shall not inherit the kingdom of God? Be not deceived." (1 Cor. 6:9) "Little children, let no man deceive you: he that doeth righteousness is righteous, even as he is righteous. He that doeth sin is of the devil." (1 John 3:7-8)

It is a fact that the great preachers of the past, the preachers whose preaching has accomplished its end, have been *preachers of righteousness.*

John Wesley, whose success in the ministry of the Word perhaps exceeds that of any other preacher since the days of the apostles, has this to say: "If we duly join faith and works in all our preaching, we shall not fail of blessing. But of all preaching, what is usually called gospel preaching is the most useless, if not the most mischievous; a dull, yea or lively, harangue on the sufferings of Christ or salvation by faith without strongly inculcating holiness. I see more and more that this naturally tends to drive holiness out of the world."[4]

Charles G. Finney says, "You must be willing to give up all your sins, and be saved from them, all, now and henceforth! Until you consent to this, you cannot be saved at all. Many would be willing to be saved in heaven, if they might hold on to some sins while on earth—or rather they think they would like heaven on such terms.

"But the fact is, they would as much dislike a pure heart and a holy life in heaven as they do on earth, and they deceive themselves utterly in supposing that they are ready or even willing to go to such a heaven as God has prepared for His people. No, there can be no heaven except for those who accept a salvation from all sin in this world. They must take the gospel as a system which holds no compromise with sin—which contemplates full deliverance from sin even now, and makes provision accordingly. Any other gospel is not the true one, and to accept of Christ's gospel in any other sense is not to accept it all. Its first and its last condition is sworn and eternal renunciation of all sin."[5]

D.L. Moody says, "There is no such thing as a man getting to heaven until he repents. You may preach Christ and offer Christ, but man has got to turn away from his sin first, as we tried to show you last night, 'Let the wicked forsake his way, the unrighteous man his thoughts, and turn unto the Lord.' Repentance is turning."[6]

Elsewhere he says, "There is one thing you cannot do, unrepentant sinner: you cannot go into the kingdom of God. You can come here; you can get into the church; but you will never get into the kingdom of God without repentance.

"God is very merciful; he is full of love, and he can pardon me. Well, you can go on in that faith, in that delusion if you like—but God says that if you don't repent *you must die*. God is true; he does not say that which is false. You can make light of it, young man or young woman, if you wish to, but the time is coming when, if you have not repented, there will not be much hope for you. You must be faithful; you must banish everything that is not good and holy."[7]

Charles Wesley, though now generally known only as a hymn writer, was nevertheless one of the most powerful and useful of preachers. He wrote in his journal, "I preached in the wood on that dreadful word, 'Sell all,' never with more assistance. How has the devil baffled those teachers, who for fear of setting men upon works, forbear urging this first universal duty! If enforcing Christ's own words is to preach works, I hope I shall preach works as long as I live."[8]

But we live in an evil day, when the devil has thus baffled most preachers; when people are more afraid of righteousness than they are of sin—more afraid of "good works" than they are of evil works; when, by subtle refinements and dispensational distinctions, half of the Word of God is made void.

The words of Christ in particular are thus made void, and it is regarded as *inexcusable legalism* to preach what he preached.

Yet Paul writes, "If any man teach otherwise, and consent not to wholesome words, even the words of our Lord Jesus Christ, and to the doctrine which is according to godliness, he is proud, knowing nothing." (1 Tim. 6:3-4) Three things are here equated: wholesome (or sound) words, the words of our Lord Jesus Christ (as recorded, of course, in the Gospels), and the doctrine which is according to godliness.

That doctrine which ignores or sets aside the words of the Lord Jesus Christ (on dispensational or other grounds) is not wholesome doctrine, nor is it the doctrine which is according to godliness. It does not promote godliness. It does not promote deep and solid work in the souls of men. And observe, the doctrine which is according to godliness is that which insists upon godliness as essential to salvation.

This is without question the great burden of "the words of our Lord Jesus Christ," which is the very reason that so many are so anxious to allocate them to a bygone dispensation. For he preached that if men do not forgive others, God will not forgive them; that if we love our life, we shall lose it, but that if we hate our life in this world, we shall keep it unto life eternal; that none shall enter the kingdom of heaven but those who do the will of the Father; and many such like things. Who preaches such things today? Yet this only is sound doctrine, and this only is calculated to perform solid and permanent work in the souls of men.

That preaching which is so common today, which ignores or denies all of this, which knows no terms of salvation but "accept Christ as your Savior" (a thing the Bible never mentions), is not "the doctrine which is according to godliness." It does not promote righteousness, but carelessness and sin. It does not awaken souls, but deceives and deludes them.

How desperately do we need a return to the preaching of righteousness!

Judgment

The Bible is full, from beginning to end, of "the judgment of God." Yet how little does the world believe in it!

For six millenniums the devil has been preaching one message: "Ye shall not surely die!" That is to say, "You can sin, and get away with it. God is loving and forgiving, and will not call you to account for it. Christ died for your sins, and therefore you may live in your sins, and go to heaven at the last. Sin today, 'confess' tomorrow, and live happily ever after!" And how has the devil deceived the world! What droves of *professing* Christians have embraced his lies!

How little preaching do we hear today of the certain judgment of God against sin! The Lord himself preached often about hell, and in the most solemn and awful words: "tormented in this flame"—"where their worm dieth not and their fire is not quenched"—"outer darkness" weeping and gnashing of teeth"—"unquenchable fire"—"everlasting fire." Elsewhere we read, "They shall be tormented day and night for ever and ever."

Oh, to get a vision of what hell is! How this would open the floodgates in our souls of earnestness, of eloquence, of tears, of powerful pleading. "Knowing the terror of the Lord," says Paul, "we persuade men." If only the world could be brought to a conviction of the reality, the certainty, and the severity of the judgment of God, how would souls be swept into the kingdom of God. Preacher, *preach the judgment of God!*

The Wonderful Cross

But beyond all of this, we have to preach what may properly be called the *gospel*—the unsearchable riches of Christ—the tender, melting, wooing, winning love of God. The former truths may break down a hardened sinner; *the love of God will melt and win him.* If ever a man effectually used the Word of God as a hammer to break hardened hearts in pieces, that man was Charles G. Finney. Yet of him we read, "Like the apostle John, President Finney made love the principal theme of his old age. He could hardly refer to the love of God without weeping."[9]

Finney himself says, "It is a matter of fact, that this manifestation of God in Christ does break the heart of sinners. It has subdued many hearts, and will thousands more . . . Certainly, if you saw it as it is, and felt the force of it in your heart, you would sob out on your very seat, break down and cry out—*Did Jesus love me so? And shall I love sin any more?* Ah, your heart would melt as thousands have been broken and melted in every age, when they have seen the love of Jesus as revealed on the cross."[10]

I do not intend to dwell upon this side of the message, for the fact is, in our day there is generally a one-sided emphasis upon the love and grace of God, to the neglect of His righteousness, holiness, and judgment. It is true, "God is love," but it is also true that "God is light," yea, and "a consuming fire." That only is sound doctrine which takes full account of both sides of God's nature, and both sides of His revelation. This makes sound theology, and this makes useful preaching.

The great John Wesley wrote to one of his preachers, "I see a danger you are in, which perhaps you do not see yourself. Is it not most pleasing to me as well as to you to be always preaching the love of God? And is there not a time when we are peculiarly led thereto, and find a peculiar blessing therein? Without doubt so it is. But yet it would be utterly wrong and unscriptural to preach nothing else. Let the law always prepare for the gospel. I scarce ever spoke more earnestly here of the love of God in Christ than last night; but it was after I had been tearing the unawakened in pieces. Go thou and do likewise."[11]

Elsewhere he says, "I think the right method of preaching is this: at our first beginning to preach at any place, after a general declaration of the love of God to sinners and His willingness that they should be saved, to preach the law in the strongest, the closest, the most searching manner possible; only intermixing the gospel here and there, and showing it, as it were, afar off.

"After more and more persons are convinced of sin, we may mix more and more of the gospel, in order to beget faith, to raise into spiritual life those whom the law hath slain; but this is not to be done too hastily neither. Therefore it is not expedient wholly to omit the law; not only because we may well suppose that many of our hearers are still unconvinced, but because there is danger that many who are convinced will heal their own wounds slightly: therefore it is only in private converse with a thoroughly convinced sinner that we should preach nothing but the gospel."[12]

But at this point many preachers may say, "That is all very well for an evangelist, but I am not an evangelist. It is not my business to save the lost, but to edify the saved." To such I must address a few words. To begin with, I fear that this is too often an excuse for lack of power and fruitfulness.

It is the business of every saint to *hold forth the Word of life*: how much more, then, of those who are engaged in the public ministry of the Word? It is an easy thing, when we see no souls saved , to say, "This is not my gift. My gift is to edify the saints." For edification is a difficult thing to measure or count. We may easily persuade ourselves that we are accomplishing our mission, when in fact we are accomplishing little or nothing.

I am persuaded that the preaching which does not much convert sinners does not much edify saints either.

Is not this the plain import of the following words of the apostle Paul? "But prophesying serveth not for them that believe not, but for them that believe," and "he that prophesieth edifieth the church." (1 Cor. 14:22,4)

Nevertheless, of that same ministry which is for the profit and edification of the church, he also tells us, "But if all prophesy, and there come in one that believeth not, or one unlearned, he is convinced (convicted—the same word as in John 16:8) of all, he is judged of all: and thus are the secrets of his heart made manifest, and so falling down on his face he will worship God, and report that God is in you of a truth." (Verses 24&25)

The implication here is inescapable: ministry which really edifies the church also really convicts and converts sinners.

This Scripture also implies that good preaching not only imparts instruction about God or His works, but makes His presence felt. That is the sort of preaching which both edifies the church, and convicts and converts sinners.

Oswald J. Smith says, "There are men who feel they have special talents for the edification of believers, and so they give themselves entirely to building up Christians in the Faith. This was where I was sidetracked. I felt that I had special gifts for teaching and speaking to young Christians on the Deeper Life, and so I prepared a number of addresses with the idea of devoting my time to this work, until God mercifully opened my eyes and showed me how far I was astray. There is nothing that will deepen Christian experience, edify believers and build them up in the Faith, so rapidly and thoroughly as seeing souls saved. Deep Holy Spirit meetings, where the power of God is working mightily in the conviction and Salvation of sinners, will do more for Christians than the teaching of years without it."[13]

C.H. Spurgeon says, "I now think I am bound never to preach a sermon without preaching to sinners. I do think that a minister who can preach a sermon without addressing sinners does not know how to preach."[14]

But some preachers may say, "It would be useless for me to preach to sinners, for there are generally none present. I am generally preaching to congregations made up of believers only." Indeed! And could you ask for a truer indication that your preaching *is not what it ought to be?*

For first, the preaching of the Word of God in the power of the Holy Ghost is a great drawing power. Of that we shall speak further on. But further, if those saints to whom you have been preaching were indeed edified, as they ought to be, they would be out after the lost! I have seen quite enough of such congregations of *saints only*—sometimes whole congregations of gray haired saints—who have not been able to win so much as their own children. But the real fact is, there may be a great deal more occasion for you to preach to sinners than you are aware of.

So many preachers, for so long a time, have been daubing with untempered mortar—by their failure to preach repentance and righteousness. I am persuaded the membership of many evangelical and fundamental churches is made up largely of persons who are in fact *unconverted*, whatever their profession may be. Is not their loose and worldly way of life, their lack of relish for the things of God, their failure even to attend most of the meetings of the church, an indication of this?

We readily grant that there is plenty of occasion for us to preach to Christians also. Alas! Altogether too much occasion. "Is it not time something was done?" says Charles G. Finney. "Is it not time that some church struck out a path, that should not be conformed to the world, but should be according to the example and spirit of Christ?

"You profess that you want to have sinners converted. But what avails it, if they sink right back again into conformity with the world? Brethren, I confess, I am filled with pain in view of [the] conduct of the church. Where are the proper results of the glorious revivals we have had? I believe they were genuine revivals of religion, and outpourings of the Holy Ghost, that the church has enjoyed the last ten years. I believe the converts of the last ten years are among the best Christians in the land. Yet after all, the great body of them are a *disgrace* to religion.

"Of what use would it be to have a thousand members added to the church, to be just such as are now in it? Would religion be any more honored by it, in the estimation of ungodly men? One holy church, that are really crucified to the world, and the world to them, would do more to recommend Christianity than all the churches in the country, living as they now do.

"O, if I had strength of body, to go through the churches again, instead of preaching to convert sinners, I would preach to bring up the churches to the gospel standard of holy living! Of what use is it to convert sinners, and make them such Christians as these?"[15]

These words are all too true—and more so today than they were a hundred and fifty years ago, when Finney preached them. In the light of this, it is not difficult to determine what should be the matter of our preaching to the people of God. We must labor to bring them into the spirit and power of New Testament Christianity. We must set their souls to thirst for the real Christianity of the New Testament—namely, that they walk as Christ walked (1 John 2:6); that they be perfect as their Father in heaven is perfect (Matt. 5:48); that they stand perfect and complete in all the will of God (Col. 4:12); that they be filled with all joy and peace in believing (Rom. 15:13); that they always abound in the work of the Lord (1Cor. 15:58); that they exhort one another daily (Heb. 3:13): that they be filled with all the fullness of God (Eph. 3:19); that they live more than conquerors in the midst of tribulation, distress, persecution, famine, nakedness, peril, and sword (Rom. 8:35-37)—and we could go on and on. Here is the spirit of real New Testament Christianity.

But alas, these are the very notes that are seldom heard in modern preaching. But let a man preach these things, not as dry doctrines, but as living realities which grip his own soul, and saints will really be edified, and sinners really converted.

The Manner of Good Preaching

We must move on to the *manner* of our preaching, having spent already a good deal more time than I had intended upon the *matter* of it. And the manner, indeed, I judge to be of greater importance than the matter. I do not mean that it is acceptable to preach what is wrong; but a man may preach what is right, and yet preach it in such a manner as to do no good by it. He may preach the truth, and yet in such a dull, dry, lukewarm, and half-hearted manner, that if it accomplishes anything at all, it will only be to put people to sleep.

On the other hand, a man may be very ignorant, and yet if he has gathered some little bit of convicting, saving truth through his own experience, and preaches that bit of truth in the proper manner, he will do good by it, and it may be a great deal of good.

C. H. Spurgeon says, [they] "brought many souls to the Savior through the earnestness with which they delivered their message. There was positively nothing in their sermons (until "I have seen and heard some who were very poor preachers, who yet the provision merchant used them to wrap round his butter), yet those feeble sermons brought many to Christ. It was not what the preachers said, so much as *how they said it*, that carried conviction to the hearts of their hearers. The simplest truth was so driven home by the intensity of the utterance, and emotion of the man from whom it came, that it told with surprising effect."[16]

Numerous examples could be cited in illustration of this, but the better to establish the point, I shall limit myself to the relation of the two most extreme cases which I have come across.

Bud Robinson, who was one of the charter members of the Church of the Nazarene (founded in 1908), and whose ministry (more than that of any other man) carried the work to success, was born in a log cabin with a dirt floor in the hills of Tennessee. He was brought up in a home of drunkards, in the lowest depths of poverty. He was wholly illiterate, stuttered so badly that he could scarcely give his name when asked, was subject to frequent epileptic fits, and was an infidel. In that condition he went to a camp meeting and was gloriously converted.

The same night, lying out under the wagon, looking up at the stars—too happy to sleep—God called Bud to preach.

He shortly afterward applied for a license to preach in the Methodist Church, and they (not wishing to discourage him, and supposing that if he could do no good, he could do no harm either) reluctantly granted him one. At the next quarterly conference he reported sixty conversions.

One who knew him says, "In those early days I have seen him standing upon the platform in all his uncouthness of dress and person, stammering and stuttering in intense eagerness to speak, until he would fall prone upon the floor, foaming at the mouth, unconscious. Again and again I have seen him stand with tears streaming down his face, unable to say but six words, 'Come to Jesus. He loves you.' And the people would come, filling the altar with seekers."[17]

Subsequently, "God healed his epilepsy, healed his stammering, and unloosed his tongue—until he became one of the most sought-after and loved speakers that America has produced."[18]

Nevertheless, he had the power of God to convert sinners before any of this came about—when he could only stammer out six words.

The other case I have to relate is more remarkable still. It is told by David Marks, himself a preacher of great power and fruitfulness. "Having retired from the assembly a small distance, I heard a very singular sound in the barn where they were convened, that excited anxiety and alarm. I returned in haste; and on entering the meeting, saw a young man standing before the assembly in a flood of tears; who, by signs and gestures, was attempting to describe the joys of heaven, and the horrors of hell. The sound of his voice was inarticulate, but varied with his signs to express happiness and misery. The whole assembly was deeply affected; to my astonishment, I found that this young man, though deaf and dumb, had opened his mouth to persuade the wicked from the way to hell.

"He had lately experienced a hope in God, and related his experience by signs; showing his fears of punishment by looking at the fire, and then pointing downward; and his views of heaven, by touching things that were bright, or of the color of gold, and pointing upward.

"He desired and received baptism, and became a faithful member of the church. The exercises of the meeting appeared to interest him, as much as any one; and though he could neither hear words nor articulate them, yet he had sounds peculiar to exhortation, prayer, and singing, accompanied by suitable gestures. I understood his public exercises had been blessed to the conversion of several."[19]

Marks refers again to the same young man some years later, this time preaching at a large quarterly meeting: "His inarticulate sounds, his flood of tears and his earnest gestures, greatly affected the assembly, and the hardest hearts appeared to feel."[20]

Now if such preachers as these can win souls, does it no behoove those of us who cannot do so, while we are in full possession of all the faculties of mind and body, and of a (supposedly) full biblical and theological education, to hang our heads for very shame? But I forget myself. I have related these examples to show that the *manner of our preaching* is of greater weight than the matter.

How then should we preach? Without pretending to exhaust the subject, I answer: with *authority*, with *simplicity*, with *earnestness*, with *solemnity*, and with *love*.

Authority

Of him who spoke as never man spoke we read, "And they were astonished at his doctrine, for he taught them as one that had authority, and not as the scribes." (Mark 1:22)

One thing is plain here: the words of Christ went home to the hearts of His hearers. They were astonished (or amazed) at His teaching. It was altogether different from the common teaching of the day. It was with authority.

And may we not discover here one great reason why the preaching of the present day makes so little impression upon the hearers? Men do not speak with authority, though they have an infallible book in their hands. They tamely suggest, rather than powerfully proclaim. They preach opinions or "interpretations," rather than certain truth which is known and felt in the bottom of their own souls. For one reason or another, whether it be lukewarmness, lack of a single eye, or some other cause, men lack deep and solid convictions of truth in their own souls.

Their preaching is, therefore, without conviction, and makes little impression upon the hearers. The trumpet gives an uncertain sound, and none are moved by it. They preach about Paul and the Corinthians, or about Christ and the Pharisees, but do not take the Word of God as a two-edged sword, or a hammer that breaks the rock in pieces; they do not drive the living, burning message of God into the souls of the people before them.

Martin Luther shook Christendom because he spoke with authority. By this means he opposed, and shook to its foundations, that church which claimed to be the sole repository of the authority of God. If Luther had not spoken with authority, he could have made no impression at all. He spoke with authority because he had rock-solid convictions in his own soul.

The test of conviction is this: if a man can hold his doctrine alone, in the face of the whole world (and the whole church too), and if he will give his life for it, it is worthy to bear the name of *conviction*.

And such was Luther's doctrine to Luther. Says he, "I am sure that my doctrines proceed from heaven. I have made them triumph against him who, in his little finger, has more force and cunning than all the popes, all the kings, and all the doctors that ever were. My dogmas will stand, and the pope will fall, despite all the gates of hell, all the powers of the air, of the earth, of the sea."[21] Such statements abound in the writings of Luther.

Now a man who has such convictions of truth in his own soul will speak with authority. If he has them not, he will not speak with authority, no matter how hard he may try to do so, and his preaching will take little effect in the hearts of his hearers. We would just hint at this point, that in this particular, as well as others of which we shall speak, a man's preaching will be a true reflection of the man himself. "A good man, out of the good treasure of the heart, bringeth forth good things." (Matt. 12:35) He cannot rise above what he himself is. What he is will determine the worth of his preaching. We shall have more to say of that further along.

Paul preached "not with enticing words of man's wisdom." (1 Cor. 2:4) Early in the career of Girolamo Savonarola, the great Italian of the fifteenth century, one of his own disciples advised him that his manner of preaching did not favorably compare with that of a great (but now forgotten) orator of the time. "To which Savonarola made reply, almost in anger, 'These verbal elegancies and ornaments will have to give way to sound doctrine simply preached.'"[22]

Savonarola did not desire to impress the people with his preaching, but with the truth. And by means of *"sound doctrine simply preached"* he became one of the most eloquent and powerful preachers of all time.

C. H. Spurgeon once said, "I hate oratory. I come down as low as I can. High-flying and fine language seems to me wicked when souls are perishing."[23]

Of D. L. Moody it was said by A. T. Pierson, "He had learned to preach simply—let us rather say he had not learned to preach otherwise; and in the unaffected language of nature, uncorrupted by the fastidious culture of the schools, he spoke face-to-face with men; and they heard him."[24]

Indeed, were it not for "the fastidious culture of the schools," there would be very little necessity to speak at all on the subject. But the ministerial schools, while they design to teach men how to preach, in fact *effect the reverse*. Charles G. Finney says, "I am still solemnly impressed with the conviction that the schools are, to a great extent, spoiling the ministers. Ministers in these days have great facilities for obtaining information on all theological questions; and are vastly more learned, so far as theological, historical, and biblical learning is concerned, than they perhaps ever have been in any age of the world. Yet with all their learning, they do not know how to use it. They are, after all, to a great extent, like David in Saul's armor."[25]

"Saul's armor" is precisely what we are dealing with here—whether it be called elocution, rhetoric, homiletics, or "the art of preaching." It is "the wisdom of words." It is not the "demonstration of the Spirit and of power," nor is it able to contribute a whit towards the procuring of it.

Where was Peter's alliterated outline when three thousand souls were cut to the heart and converted to Christ by an unpremeditated address? This was the demonstration of the Spirit and of power, and again I affirm that all of men's education in the "wisdom of words" and the "excellency of speech" cannot begin to procure it.

So far as these things affect the matter at all, they defeat their own design. They put the armor of Saul upon the man of faith, and so far from enabling him, it encumbers him.

If the young men of our day were experienced in the ways of God as David was, if they had learned (as David had) the efficacy of faith and the power of God, they would reject the armor of Saul as David did, as both unnecessary and detrimental. It puts the *wisdom of men* in the place of the *power of God*.

But beyond that, it is also a plain fact that the refinements of art—"the fastidious culture of the schools"—can never move the masses as can the simplicity of nature. And if we do not preach to move people, what do we preach for? Polished orators tickle the ears of the cultured for a few years, and then are forgotten. But plain and simple men who preach not with wisdom of words, but with the demonstration of the Spirit and of power, move the masses, and their names are immortal.

Such men were John Bunyan, Christmas Evans, D. L. Moody, C. H. Spurgeon, Gipsy Smith and Billy

Sunday—not one of whom possessed an iota of "higher education," or of "ministerial education."

John Bunyan's preaching, though the epitome of simplicity, was both powerful and fruitful. The learned John Owen used to go to hear him when he preached in London. "Charles II once asked him, in wonder; how a courtly man such as he was could sit and listen to an illiterate tinker. 'May it please your Majesty,' said Owen, 'could I possess that tinker's abilities for preaching, I would gladly relinquish all my learning.'"[26] I suppose he little dreamed that that may have been exactly what it would have cost him.

Earnestness

Good preaching is that which comes from the heart. It is that which is born of feeling and bathed with tears. And here we have come to the core of the whole matter. *Earnest* emotion—heart feeling—is the great desideratum in preaching. Without this, however good in other respects, preaching will do but little good. But where this is found, it will go far to make amends for every other kind of deficiency.

Have we not abundantly demonstrated this in the two examples cited above—of Bud Robinson convicting and converting sinners by stammering out six words, "with tears streaming down his face," and of a deaf and dumb man winning souls by inarticulate sounds, signs, and gestures, with a flood of tears? Here indeed is the core of the whole matter; I believe that the *absence of tears* from the preaching of the present day is the surest indication of the weakness and unprofitableness thereof.

Paul "ceased not to warn every one night and day with tears." (Acts 20:31) He wrote to the Corinthians "out of much affliction and anguish of heart," and "with many tears." (2 Cor. 2:4) He wrote to the Philippians "even weeping." (Phil. 3:18) He *felt* what he preached, and therefore he made others feel it. He was moved by the truths which he handled, moved to the bottom of his heart and soul, and therefore he moved others.

Here is the secret of good preaching, of great preaching, of powerful preaching, of useful preaching: the promise of success is to him "that goeth forth and weepeth, bearing precious seed." He "shall doubtless come again with rejoicing, bringing his sheaves with him." (Psalm 126:6)

We are often told (by unfruitful preachers) that God does not require us to be successful, only to be faithful. Is not this another excuse for lukewarmness? God has promised success to the earnest, fervent man—to the man who preaches with tears. And if we are not thus earnest and fervent, are we faithful?

When Christ sent forth the twelve, he "gave them power and authority over all devils, and to cure diseases." (Luke 9:1) Yet when an actual case came before them (verse 40), they were powerless, and could not cast out the demon. What a poor plea it had been in their mouth to say, "We are not required to be successful, only to be faithful"! If they had been faithful, they would have been successful. "O faithless and perverse generation", saith the Lord; and when they asked him why they could not cast him out, he said, "Because of your unbelief." (Matt. 17:20) If they had faith in the Word of Christ, if they had been earnest and fervent, if they had given themselves to prayer and fasting, they would have been successful.

It is a plain fact that the successful preachers have generally been the earnest preachers, and (though there are other factors that enter into the matter) the greater the fervency of a man, the greater has been his fruitfulness.

George Whitefield was probably the greatest preacher who has walked the earth since the days of the apostles. What made him so? His sermons were preached extemporaneously, often unpremeditated, and he "knew nothing of such a kind of exercise as the planning of a sermon."[27] So says Cornelius Winter, who lived under his roof for a year and a half.

His printed sermons are inferior in matter to those of many other preachers, yet when he preached them, the "rambling effusions: (as some have called them) excelled all others, and were freighted with the demonstration of the Spirit and of power. How so? Cornelius Winter says further, "I hardly ever knew him go through a sermon without weeping, and I believe his were the tears of sincerity. His voice was often interrupted by his affection; and I have heard him say in the pulpit, 'You blame me for weeping, but how can I help it, when you will not weep for yourselves, though your souls are on the verge of destruction, and for aught I know, you are hearing your last sermon!' Sometimes he wept exceedingly, stamped loudly and passionately, and was frequently so overcome, that nature required some little time to compose itself."[28]

Is it any wonder that such preaching went home to the hearts of the people? A careless young man who heard Whitefield for the first time thus describes the manner and effects of his preaching: "Mr. Whitefield described the Sadducean character—this did not touch me. I thought myself as good a Christian as any man in England. From this he went to that of the

Pharisees. He described their exterior decency, but observed that the poison of the viper rankled in their hearts. This rather shook me. At length, in the course of his sermon, he abruptly broke off; paused for a few moments; then burst into a flood of tears; lifted up his hands and eyes, and exclaimed, 'O my hearers! The wrath's to come! The wrath's to come!'

"These words sunk into my heart, like lead in the waters. I wept, and when the sermon was ended, retired alone.

"For days and weeks I could think of little else. Those awful words would follow me, wherever I went, 'The wrath's to come! The wrath's to come!' "[29] The young man was soon converted, and afterwards became a preacher.

Charles Wesley also preached without premeditation, sometimes opening his Bible and preaching from the first text that presented itself. Of him we read, "His discourses from the pulpit were not dry and systematic, but flowed from the present views and feelings of his own mind. He had a remarkable talent of expressing the most important truths with simplicity and energy; and his discourses were sometimes truly apostolic, forcing conviction on the hearers in spite of the most determined opposition."[30]

Another who knew him well writes, "His ministerial gift was in one respect truly extraordinary: it came the nearest of any thing I ever witnessed to that which we have reason to believe was the original way to preaching the gospel...where only God and conscious sinner were before him, it seemed as if nothing could withstand the wisdom and power with which he spake: to use the expression of a pious man, 'It was all thunder and lightning.'"[31]

Plainly this cannot be attributed to any principles of homiletics, for homiletics never did produce such preaching, and Charles Wesley used no homiletics. What then? He was a man fervent in spirit, as his whole life testifies. His preaching was, above all things, earnest. He preached *from the heart,* and was often suffused with tears while he spoke. Here is his own simple explanation of his power: "I felt every word I spoke this morning. What comes from the heart usually goes to the heart."[32]

The power of Charles G. Finney is well known. Of his preaching one says, "His sermons were chain lightning, flashing conviction into the hearts of the stoutest skeptics."[33] Of his earnest emotion we read, "He could thunder the terrors of the law with appalling power, and then turn and offer the mercy of the gospel with the tenderness and tears of Jeremiah or Christ."[34]

Finney thus describes his own preaching: "I had my pocket Bible in my hand, and read to them this text: 'God so loved the world that he gave his only begotten son, that whosoever believeth in him might not perish, but have everlasting life.'

"I cannot remember much that I said; but I know that the point on which my mind principally labored was the treatment which God received in return for His love. The subject affected my own mind very much and I preached and poured our my soul and my tears together." "Indeed I let loose my whole heart upon them." "Indeed it seemed to myself as if I could rain hail and love upon them at the same time."[35]

It is unnecessary to multiply examples. All the great preachers have been earnest preachers, and weeping was once as common in the pulpit as laughing is today. "O those tears, those tears," says John Angell James, "how they reprove us for insensibility, and how they prove to us our deficiencies."[36]

C. H. Spurgeon says, "I hope I am not wrong in supposing that all of us are thoroughly sincere in our Master's service; so I will go on to what seems to me to be the next qualification, manward, for soul winning, and that is *evident earnestness* . . . if a man is to be a soul-winner, there must be in him intensity of emotion as well as sincerity of heart. You may preach the most solemn warnings, and the most dreadful threatening, in such an indifferent or careless way that no one will be in the least affected by them; and you may repeat the most affectionate exhortations in such a half-hearted manner that no one will be moved either to love or fear. I believe, brethren, that for soul-wining there is more in this matter of earnestness than in almost anything else."[37]

I do not wish to be misunderstood in thus ascribing power to earnestness, as though I would dispense with the necessity of the *unction of the Holy Ghost.* Not for a moment. But I believe that the Spirit of God uses proper tools.

A man does not use a hammer to cut down a tree. No more does God use a lukewarm, half-hearted preacher to convert sinners. I do not mean that God cannot use such a preacher at all; but he will not use him very much. He will not do by him what he will do by an earnest, fervent man.

If I am desperate to cut down a tree, and can get my hands on no tool but a hammer, I could make shift to get the tree down by chopping with the hammer. But I would not cut down very many trees by such a method, nor very big ones! And just so will God use a dull preacher to convert sinners. He may win a few here and there—but the hard cases he will not touch at all. Where God has a work to do, he comes looking for a man who is fit for the task. Where he finds none, the work cannot be done, and he pours out judgment instead of mercy. (Ezek. 22: 30-31)

The power of the Holy Spirit is no substitute for a holy, earnest, fervent man. He comes upon the man, anoints him, and fills him—not to set aside the powers and faculties of the man, but to use them.

Solemnity

Solemnity, or *seriousness*, is closely allied to earnestness. It may be that solemnity is only a particular form of earnestness. I shall not attempt to determine that. I believe it is distinct enough, and important enough, to receive a separate treatment.

The themes which occupy a preacher of the Word of God ought to inspire him with the deepest solemnity. *God! Immortally! Sin! Holiness! Judgment! Eternity!* Surely there is no room for trifling here, and it is shameful—exceeding shameful—that there is so much joking and laughing in the pulpit today.

There will be no laughing when *jesting preachers* stand before God to give account of all of their idle words, and of the solemn opportunities—with congregations of dying sinners before them—which they have thus trifled away.

We would not exclude laughter altogether, neither from the pulpit nor from life. There is "a time to weep, and a time to laugh." (Eccl. 3:4) Nevertheless, in this world of sin and sorrow, weeping will always take the precedence in those who walk with God. We read, "Blessed are they that mourn"—but never "Blessed are they that laugh." Nay, we are told, "Woe unto you that laugh now! For ye shall mourn and weep." (Luke 6:25)

We read often that Christ and His apostles wept—never that they laughed. It is certain that their preaching was not filled with the foolishness which is so common in the pulpit today. This is neither for the glory of God nor the good of souls.

However, the absence of joking and laughing from a man's preaching is no sign that he is solemn. Solemnity will rest upon the spirit of a man who stands in the presence of eternity, and feels intensely its awful realities.

C. H. Spurgeon says, "Something of the shadow of the last tremendous day must fall upon our spirit and give the accent of conviction to our message of mercy, or we shall miss the pleader's true power . . .

"He that pleads for Christ should himself be moved with the prospect of the judgment day. When I come in at yonder door, at the back of the pulpit, and the sight of that vast crowd bursts upon me, I frequently feel appalled. Think of these thousands of immortal souls gazing through the windows of those wistful eyes, and I am to preach to them all, and be responsible for their blood if I be not faithful to them. I tell you, it makes me feel ready to start back."[38]

This, beloved, is the sort of solemnity of which we speak. A man who feels thus will naturally communicate that feeling to his hearers.

Thus we read of John Wesley: "Mr. Wesley preached in the church, to a numerous congregation, serious as the grave! While he spent fifty-eight minutes enforcing that awful passage in the second lesson, respecting Dives and Lazarus, he could hardly give over praying in his sermon. O! how much was he affected! [39]

The preaching of Jonathan Edwards was characterized by the deepest solemnity, and that solemnity served to compensate for grave deficiencies in other particulars. He had been taught to preach in a manner that can hardly be called preaching at all: he wrote his sermons out, and read them to the people—and that apparently with no fervency or animation. His biography says, "He wrote his sermons, and in so fine and illegible a hand that they could be read only by being brought near to the eye . . . While preaching, he customarily stood, holding his small manuscript volume in his left hand, the elbow resting on the cushion or the Bible, his right hand rarely raised but to turn the leaves, and his person almost motionless."[40]

We read further, "He had no studied varieties of the voice, and no strong emphasis. He scarcely gestured, or even moved."[41] As to his matter, though, "From the first step to the last, he aimed at nothing but the salvation of his hearers."[42] And though he dwelt heavily upon sin and righteousness and judgment, yet he was "certainly not a little wanting in the tenderness and melting pathos of the gospel of salvation."[43]

Yet for all of these deficiencies, his preaching took hold of the people in a remarkable way. We read such things as the following of its effects: "There was scarcely a single person in the town, either old or young, that was felt unconcerned about the great things of the eternal world. Those that were wont to be the vainest, and loosest, and those that had been most disposed to think and speak slightly of vital and experimental religion, were now generally subject to great awakenings. And the work of conversion was carried on in a most astonishing manner, and increased more and more; souls did, as it were, come by flocks to Jesus Christ."[44]

On the human side of things, we can account for such results upon no other ground than that of the intense solemnity which characterized all of his preaching. He felt realities of eternity, and so made others feel them. His biography says, "His appearance in the pulpit was with a good grace, and his delivery easy, perfectly natural, and very solemn."[45]

Another writes of him, "A remarkable instance of conviction also has been sometimes under the ministry of the Rev. Mr. Edwards of Northampton: a preacher of a low and moderate voice, a natural way of delivery, and without any agitation of body, or any thing else in the manner to excite attention, except his habitual and great solemnity, looking and speaking as in the presence of God, with a weighty sense of the matter delivered."[46]

Love

There is no power on earth like that of *love*. Love will win and conquer where all else has failed. Cultist, infidels, Jews, and hardened and careless sinners of every sort will feel the power of love.

"In a large gathering of Christian Jews, ninety-three percent of them testified that they were aroused to consider the claims of Jesus Christ because some Gentile Christian had shown them love."[47]

I venture to offer, as an illustration to this, my own experience, quoted from my journal: I came to one house, where were three young men and one girl, evidently students. I stayed near two hours, but it was a dreary and profitless argument—the girl especially strongly opposing all that I could say. But somehow we fell upon the subject of persecution, at which she said, "If you want to see persecution, look at the history of the Jews."

I looked her in the eyes and asked (what I suspected), "Are you a Jew?"

She said, "Yes."

I said, "I know the history of the Jews, and when I read it I weep." I paused, and the tears began to run down my face—but I continued looking her in the eye, and said, "I love Jews. And Christ loves Jews." By this she was overcome, and ran out of the room as fast as she could, closing the door behind her. I might add to this, what I neglected to record at the time, that when I thus spoke to her, she burst into tears herself, and covered her face with both of her hands to hide them, while she ran from the room.

Whether she was ever converted, I am not able to say, for I never saw her again. But I record this as an example of the power of love to move the heart, when nothing else will do so.

When a preacher speaks from a heart filled with love, his hearers will feel and be moved by this, even though the most of them may not be able to explain what it is that moves them. In the journal of John Wesley we read: "We came to Bolton about five in the evening. We had no sooner entered the main street than we perceived the lions at Rochdale were lambs in comparison to those of Bolton.

"Such rage and bitterness I scarce ever saw before, in any creature that bore the form of men. They followed us in full cry to the house where we went; and as soon as we were gone in, took possession of all the avenues to it, and filled the street from one end to the other . . .

"Presently one ran up and told us the mob had *bursted* into the house . . . Believing the time was now come, I walked down into the thickest of them. They had now filled all the rooms below. I called for a chair. The winds were hushed, and all was calm and still. My heart was filled with love, my eyes, with tears, and my mouth with arguments. They were amazed, they were ashamed, they were melted down, they devoured every word."[48]

But, "Though I speak with the tongues of men and of angels, and have not love, I am become as sounding brass, or a tinkling cymbal." (1 Cor.13:1) I may please the ear, but I will not move the heart or win the soul.

But in this, as in the other particulars, *love must be real*. We must have the real outflow of love which really dwells in the heart. The best example of that love which I know is to be found in Samuel H. Hadley, for some years the superintendent of the Jerry McAuley Water Street Mission in New York City.

R. A. Torrey says of him, "He was the embodiment of Christlike love."[49] J. Wilbur Chapman says, "It is, however, the universal testimony of those who have been most faithful in their attendance at Water Street, that it was not simply Mr. Hadley's way of saying things, but what he was himself, that counted with the men who were ready to listen to him . . . In all my experience as a minister I have never known anyone, I am sure, who was so perfect an illustration of the love of Christ for sinful men as himself, and almost a countless number of people today rise up to call him blessed."[50]

It was the power of love which enabled him to convert hundreds of the most wicked and degraded of men and women.

Harry Monroe, of the Pacific Garden Mission in Chicago, writes, "The 13th chapter of First Corinthians has always been a gem of rare beauty to me. I have read commentaries upon it, but never fully understood its interpretation until I met S. H. Hadley at a convention of Christian workers at Tremont Temple, in Boston, November, 1892. And while others may wonder at the secret of his marvelous success, I discovered on that occasion that he possessed a passion born of God for souls that equipped him for what has proved a most remarkable ministry."[51]

Mel Trotter, of the Mel Trotter Mission in Grand Rapids, writes, "I first met S. H. Hadley at Northfield, Mass., six years ago. I heard him speak at Round Top; got down in front of him where I could see his face and the first look that I got of him my heart went out to him and I've loved him ever since.

"As he told the story of his life, I cried like a child. I had suffered from the same sin.

"At once I began to search for his power. I talked with him about his work, and about mission work generally, but did not tell him I was a mission man. I wanted to learn his methods and the secret of his power.

"In Chicago the next winter, where we were together at a Christian Worker's Convention, I saw a practical demonstration of it. I found his power lay in his love for souls—and his love of souls came from his love of Christ and the vision that comes by the baptism of the Holy Ghost; so I reasoned it this way: to love the unlovely, as S. H. Hadley does, one must have the love of God shed abroad in his heart by the Holy Ghost. "I saw him talking to a man who was drunk and slipped up close to him and listened to what he said, and he stood there and wept over the stranger that was drunk.

"I turned from him and went alone before God—and stayed there until God gave me the same power. I used to *try* to love souls, and I did win some for Jesus, but after S. H. Hadley came into my life I did not have to try; God put the love there."[52]

Whether we are preaching to saints or sinners, scarcely anything exceeds the importance of "speaking the truth in love." (Eph. 4:15)

A man may preach the truth of God, and yet be so hard and cold in it that he fails altogether to draw and warm and win the hearts of his hearers. He may actually drive them farther from God.

"There is that speaketh like the piercings of a sword, but the tongue of the wise is health." (Prov. 12:18) "The wise" are those who turn many to righteousness. (Daniel 13:3) "The wise" are those who win souls. (Prov. 11:30)

It is love which draws hearts, wins souls, and edifies saints also, for "knowledge puffs up, but love edifies." (1Cor. 8:1)

The Effects of Good Preaching

We must move on to the *effects* of good preaching. Here is the real test: however good preaching may be thought to be, if it does not accomplish its end, what is it good for?

I have often heard preachers comfort themselves with the *supposed* fact that the Word of God will not return unto him void, but will accomplish the thing where to it is sent, even though that Word as preached by them accomplishes nothing at all.

This may appear to be the language of pious faith, but in fact it is the language of *lukewarmness*. It is the language of one who is content to be unfruitful. That text of Scripture in the hands of faith would have an altogether different effect: it would drive a man to his knees, to wrestle with God with strong crying and tears, with groanings which cannot be uttered; to mend his ways; to spend and be spent, until he could see with his eyes the fruit of that word.

I have seen a Pentecostal preacher pray for healing for a woman who said she did not have a good tooth in her mouth. He pronounced her healed, though her teeth remained just what they were, and gravely informed the people that such healings need not be instantaneous, but that the work was surely being done, and before long she would have a mouth full of good teeth. Now was this the language of faith, or of folly and deception?

Yet I can detect no difference between this and the supposition of many preachers that the Word which they preach is accomplishing the purpose of God, though they see it not. Elijah *did not pray so*, but sent his servant again and again to look for the cloud, while he tarried to wrestle with God. Neither would he be content so long as the servant told him, "There is nothing." Neither would he desist until he could see with his eyes the approaching cloud. And this James calls *praying earnestly*; this he calls effectual, fervent prayer.

When we begin to see earnest, fervent preaching, we shall soon see the little cloud arising, soon the heaven black with clouds and wind, and soon the showers of blessing falling upon the parched ground.

Good preaching will *accomplish* its end. What effects, then, are we to look for?

Good Preaching Draws People

To begin with, good preaching *draws people*. "The harvest is great." "The fields are white already to harvest." Beneath the foam and froth of a life of vanity, beneath the pride and self-sufficiency of life without God, beneath the hurry of a life of pleasure, beneath the hardness of a life of sin, there lies in every man a hungry heart and an accusing conscience. "But the laborers are few." How few are the preachers who are able to penetrate through the bustle and froth and hardness and self-sufficiency, and speak to the very soul of the man! We have abundance of preachers, but few who can so wield the sword of the Spirit, as to pierce through all of the armor with which men have fortified themselves against God, and speak to the very heart and conscience. Yet I believe that the truths of sin and righteousness and judgment, and of the tender, seeking, longsuffering love of God, preached authoritatively, earnestly, and lovingly, will accomplish exactly that. And when a man arises who can preach so, the people are drawn to him.

They may not be able to understand *why* they are drawn to him, but they know and feel instinctively that he sweeps away the cobwebs from the deepest recesses of their heart and soul. He makes them feel where they have never felt before; he brings them face-to-face with those realities which touch the very core of their being, and they are powerfully, perhaps irresistibly, drawn to him.

How the people were drawn to Christ! They followed him out into the desert, and abode with him three days with nothing to eat, merely to hear the words that fell from his lips! I know he spoke as never man spoke—I know the Spirit was given to him without measure. But we may speak the same truth—by the same Spirit, according to our measure. Why shouldn't we see the same kind of results, though in lesser measure? Nay, why not even in *greater measure*? Indeed, Christ has said, "He that believeth on me, the works that I do shall he do also; and greater works than these, because I go unto my Father." (John 14:12)

How often do the men of our day explain away this Scripture by affirming that it does not apply to miraculous works, or to physical works, but only to *spiritual works?* Very well then: here is a *spiritual work* for you to do.

But we need not establish the matter thus; it is a plain fact that through all time the servants of Christ have drawn the people precisely as their Lord did. Of John the Baptist we read, "Then went out to him Jerusalem, and all Judea, and all the region round about Jordan." (Matt. 3:5)

The preachers of the present day must build elegant and comfortable "temples" in large metropolitan centers, equip them with padded pews, carpeted aisles, and air conditioning—and for all that, must use games and prizes and entertainment to draw but the smallest part of their own metropolitan population. John the Baptist had none of this. He built no "temple," and no "bus ministry." He offered no entertainment or "special music," and never spent a penny for "promotion." And yet the whole population flocked to his preaching. They "went out to him"— out into the desert, though they had no automobiles in which to get there. And they went for one thing only: to hear the Word of God preached in the power of the Holy Ghost.

We read that when Paul preached in a certain place, there "came almost the whole city together to hear the Word of God," so that "when the Jews saw the multitudes, they were filled with envy." (Acts 13:44-45) Unbelief may think that such things were only for apostles and prophets, but it is not so. The Word of God preached in the power of the Holy Ghost has always drawn multitudes of people, no matter who or what the preacher was.

The bare mention of the name George Whitefield was sufficient to draw a crowd of thousands of people at any time, at any place.

The following account was written by Nathan Cole, a farmer and carpenter in Connecticut. He was an unconverted man who tells us that the bare hearing of the power and success of Whitefield's preaching, in various places, had brought him under conviction, and for some time he had wished to hear him:

"Then on a sudden, in the morning about 8 or 9 of the clock, there came a messenger and said Mr. Whitefield preached at Hartford and Wethersfield yesterday and is to preach at Middletown this morning at ten of the clock. I was in my field at work. I dropped my tool that I had in my hand and ran home to my wife, telling her to make ready quickly to go and hear Mr. Whitefield preach at Middletown, then ran to my pasture for my horse with all might, fearing that I should be too late.

"Having my horse, I with my wife soon mounted the horse and went forward as fast as I thought the horse could bear; and when my horse got much out of breath, I would get down and put my wife on the saddle and bid her ride as fast as she could and not stop or slack for me except I bade her, and so I would run until I was much out of breath and then mount my horse again, and so I did several times to favor my horse." [Reader, observe: this is an unconverted man going to hear the gospel!]

"We improved every moment to get along as if we were fleeing for our lives, all the while fearing we should be too late to hear the sermon, for we had twelve miles to ride double, in a little more than an hour, and we went round by the upper housen parish.

"And when we came within about half a mile or a mile of the road that comes down from Hartford, Wethersfield, and Stepney to Middletown, on high land I saw before me a cloud of fog arising. I first thought it came from the great river, but as I came nearer the road I heard a noise of horses' feet coming down the road, and this cloud was a cloud of dust made by the horses' feet. It arose some rods into the air over the tops of hills and trees; and when I came within about 20 rods of the road, I could see men and horses slipping along in the cloud like shadows, and as I drew nearer it seemed like a steady stream of horses and their riders, scarcely a horse more than his length behind another, all of a lather and foam with sweat, their breath rolling out of their nostrils every jump. Every horse seemed to go with all his might to carry his rider to hear news from heaven for the saving of souls. . .

"We went down in the stream, but heard no man speak a word all the way for three miles—but every one pressing forward in great haste; and when we got to Middletown old meeting house, there was a great multitude, it was said to be 3 or 4,000 of people, assembled together . . . I turned and looked towards the Great River and saw the ferry boats running swift backward and forward bringing over loads of people, and the oars rowed nimble and quick. Everything—men, horses, and boats—seemed to be struggling for life. The land and banks over the river looked black with people and horses; all along the 12 miles I saw no man at work in his field, but all seemed to be gone."[53]

For above thirty years Whitefield preached day after day, sometimes twice or thrice in a day, and generally to many thousands of people.

For over fifty years John Wesley preached two and three times daily, and in the brief entries which he makes in his journal we constantly read of "an immense multitude"—"a huge multitude"—"thousands and thousands"—flocking together to hear his preaching. And be it understood, as often as not these multitudes were not seated in a comfortable building but standing under the open sky, yea, often standing for a hour with the rain pouring down upon their heads, to hear the man of God preach.

When C. H. Spurgeon began to preach in London, his New Park Street Chapel was soon crowded to suffocation. Arrangements were made to enlarge it, while he preached in the great Exeter Hall. But that too was crowded to suffocation, and Spurgeon wrote at that time. "I am always at it, and the people are teasing me almost to death to get me to let them hear my voice. It is strange that such a power should be in one small body to crowd Exeter Hall to suffocation, and block up the Strand, so that pedestrians have to turn down by-ways, and all other traffic is at a standstill . . . I believe I could secure a crowded audience at dead of night in a deep snow."[54] Further, "The Lord blessed the Word more and more to the conversion of the hearers, and Exeter Hall was thronged throughout the whole time of our sojourn. To return to New Park Street, enlarged though it was, resembled the attempt to put the sea into a teapot. We were more inconvenienced than ever. To turn many hundreds away was the general (if not the universal) necessity, and those who gained admission were but little better off, for the packing was dense in the extreme and the heat something terrible even to remember."[55]

D. L. Moody constantly engaged the largest buildings available for his meetings, or erected temporary buildings which would hold thousands of people. His power to draw the people may be illustrated by the following incident: He once engaged a large auditorium in Chicago for meetings at ten in the morning and three in the afternoon. This he did over the objection of almost everybody, for none expected him to be able to draw a crowd during business hours.

R. A. Torrey says, "On the first morning of the meetings I went down to the Auditorium about half an hour before the appointed time, but I went with much fear and apprehension; I thought the Auditorium would be nowhere nearly full. When I reached there, to my amazement, I found a queue of people four abreast extending from the Congress Street entrance to Wabash Avenue, then a break to let traffic through, and then another block, and so on. I went in through the back door, and there were many clamoring for entrance there. When the doors were opened at the appointed time, we had a cordon of twenty policemen to keep back the crowd, but the crowd was so great that it swept the cordon of policemen off their feet and packed eight thousand people into the building before we could get the doors shut. And I think there [were] as many left on the outside as there were in the building."[56]

R. A. Torrey also engaged the largest buildings which were available, or erected temporary ones where none large enough were available. Yet the buildings could not hold the crowds. We quote one example:

"Such crowds flocked to Philharmonic Hall, where the meetings were held, that it was necessary towards the close of the series to hold double meetings each night, the first being for women and the second for men.

"While the first service was in progress, thousands would be clamoring at the door for admittance. People would stand for an hour, four deep, all along the sides of the building—in the rain—waiting for an entrance."[57] Further, "One night, after notice was put up 'Hall Full,' great crowds still hung around the doors. Mr. Armstrong, a city missionary, went out and said to the crowd, 'The Hall is full; why don't you go home?'

"One lady standing near him said, 'Please, sir, we are waiting for somebody to faint.'

"He said, 'Surely you don't want anybody to faint , do you?'

"'No," she said, 'but they do faint in there sometimes, and I am waiting until somebody does, so that I can get their seat.'

"Her earnestness excited his curiosity, and he enquired if she was a Christian. She replied she was not. 'Well' , said he, 'I can probably get you in at the back door.' He succeeded, and she listened to the sermon.

"In the after-meeting, he noticed that that woman was one of the first to come down to the front seats and publicly confess her acceptance of Christ."[58]

Billy Sunday everywhere erected temporary wooden tabernacles, the largest of which would seat 22,000 people. Yet for all that, he never preached in a building large enough to accommodate the crowds. "We see him drawing amazing audience, not only once or twice, or several times, but day and night for weeks. We see one throng trying to get into his big tabernacle before another gets out. We see all kinds of organizations of men asking for reservations in the building. We see trainloads of people coming from neighboring towns. And he is drawing all these multitudes just when magazine writers and critics of

Christianity are declaring that the pulpit has lost its power. How many other men in America could attract such throngs week after week? Could any half-dozen of the best orators in the land put together do it? The eloquence of Webster and Clay is echoing in college halls and on political platforms, but did we ever hear that either of them kept tens of thousands of people coming to hear them through a period of ten weeks, in the same place and on the same theme?"[59]

Before leaving this subject, we must again observe that it was the *simple preaching of the Word of God* which drew all of these multitudes of people. There is a movement within the ranks of Fundamentalism which attaches great importance to crowds, and which does manage to gather fairly large crowds—at least on Sundays. But it is not by the simple preaching of the words of God. They compass land and sea, and leave no stone unturned, in searching for *ways and means* to keep the crowds coming. They are gathered together by means of contests, games, prizes, tricks, bribes, and entertainments of every sort. To all of this I solemnly protest.

If the preaching were *what it ought to be*, all such means would be uncalled for.

Some years ago I heard a sermon in advocacy of such means. The text was taken from Luke 5:18. "They sought means to bring him in." The text was used to defend every kind of "means" from kites and balloons and bubble gum, to carpeted aisles, padded pews, and grand pianos. But to begin with, the word "means" is not in the original at all, and so it appears in italics in the English version. The text says merely, "they sought to bring him in."

And if we inquire why they must *seek to bring him in*, we see that this advocacy of such *means* constitutes a positive denial of the spirit and power of this Scripture. We are told (verse 17) that "the power of the Lord was present to heal them." And for that reason alone the place was so thronged with people that they could not so much as get near the door. (Mark 2:2)

Now the plain fact is, if the power of the Lord were present in our modern churches, the multitudes would be drawn to them as they were to Christ. I recognize that the text speaks of the power of the Lord *to heal the body*. Nevertheless, the examples which we have cited above abundantly prove that where the power of the Lord is present to save souls, the multitudes are drawn by it.

"John [the Baptist] did no miracle," nor did George Whitefield, nor John Wesley, nor D. L. Moody, nor a host of others we could mention. They only preached the gospel in the power of the Holy Ghost, and the multitudes were drawn to them.

But some may ask, "Ought we not use such means to bring people in to hear the Word of God for the first time? How are they to be drawn to a man whom they have never heard?"

I answer: How were they drawn to Christ? Did he have padded pews and stained glass windows, and kites and bubble gum for the kiddies? How were they drawn out into the desert to hear John the Baptist? How were they drawn out into the fields to hear George Whitefield and John Wesley? Very simply: by the testimony of those who had heard them.

Let a man be moved by a preacher, and he will soon be talking of him to others—and in just the proportion that his own soul has been moved and blessed will he be bold and importunate in persuading others to hear him. No sooner does the woman of Samaria have her heart touched and her conscience searched by the words of Christ, no sooner does she have the springs of her being laid bare by this preacher, than off she goes to the men of the city—

her water pot forgotten now—saying, "Come, see a man that told me all things that ever I did!"

And this is always the case. The report of a good preacher is soon spread abroad, whether he wills or not. He speaks to the very soul of man, answers its profoundest questions, meets its deepest needs, and people who have been touched by such a man will not allow him to remain unknown. Good preaching draws people.

Good Preaching Moves People

But we must move on to other effects. Good preaching *moves people*. It makes them feel. It makes them weep. We have observed before that the absence of tears from the modern pulpit is one of the surest indications of its weakness and unprofitableness. No less so is the absence of tears from the modern pew.

There can be no doubt that the lack of tears in the modern church may be ascribed to the lukewarmness and apathy of the people in general, yet good preaching could alter the matter. We often read of whole congregations of people, ungodly people, including the most hardened of sinners, weeping profusely under the great preachers of the past.

George Whitefield wrote, "We scarce know what it is to have a meeting without tears." [60]

Again, "Arrows of conviction fled so thick and so fast, and such an universal weeping prevailed from one end of the congregation to the other, that good Mr. J— could not help going from seat to seat to speak, encourage, and comfort the wounded souls."[61] At another time, preaching when he was ill, as he often did, he says, "Nature (by continuing an hour in my discourse) was almost quite exhausted; but O what life! What power spread all around! All seemed to be melted, and were drowned in tears."[62]

Thomas Ranking, who afterwards became one of Wesley's itinerants, writes thus of the first time he heard Whitefield: "The sermon exceeded all the sermons I ever heard. About the middle of it, I ventured to look up, and saw all the crowds around Mr. Whitefield bathed in tears."[63]

Of the preaching of Christmas Evans we read, "The chapels and adjoin burying-grounds were crowded with hearers of a week-day, even in the middle of the harvest. I frequently preached in the open air in the evenings, and the rejoicing, singing, and praising would continue until broad light the next morning. The hearers appeared melted down in tenderness at the different meetings, so that they wept streams of tears, and cried out, in such a manner that one might suppose the whole congregation, male and female, was thoroughly dissolved by the gospel."[64]

Charles Wesley writes in his journal, "I entered upon my ministry at Weaver's-hall, and began expounding Isaiah, with much freedom and power. They were melted into tears all around."[65] Again, "I read prayers, and discoursed near two hours on the pool of Bethesda. The whole congregation were in tears."[66]

Again, "I preached repentance from Rev. 1:7: 'Behold, he cometh with clouds; and every eye shall see him.' The Lord opened my mouth to convince. His Word begins to sink into their hearts. Many were in tears on every side."[67]

Of the preaching of Savonarola we read, "Words fail to describe it; he was, as it were, swept onwards by a might beyond his own, and carried his audience with him. Men and women of every age and condition, workmen, poets, philosophers, would burst into passionate tears, while the church re-echoed with their sobs. The reporter taking notes of the sermon was obliged to write: 'At this point I was overcome by weeping and could not go on.'"[68]

His biographer tells us that many of his sermons are partially preserved, with a similar notation.

Of David Marks we read, "I had read his 'Narrative,' and regarded many of the statements contained in it, respecting the effect which almost always attended his preaching as utterly unaccountable; but when I heard him the first time . . . my incredulity entirely vanished. It was a communion season, and his subject was the Lord's Supper. It seemed to me that my soul was but a vessel of tears. I stifled my sobs until I could not refrain from weeping aloud. It was so with many."[69]

Of John Fletcher we read, "He was peculiarly assisted while he was applying those encouraging words, *Him that cometh unto me I will in no wise cast out*. The people were exceedingly affected; indeed quite melted down.

"The tears streamed so fast from the eyes of the poor colliers, that their black faces were washed by them, and almost universally streaked with white."[70]

Again, "He preached in the evening from the Second Epistle to the Thessalonians, Chapter II, verse 13. The whole congregation was dissolved in tears. He spoke like one who had but just left the converse of God and angels, and not like a human being."[71]

Francis Asbury writes, "I had gone through about two-thirds of my discourse, and was bringing the words home to the present: now, when such power descended that hundreds fell to the ground, and the house seemed to shake with the presence of God. The chapel was full of white and black, and many were without that could not get in. Look wherever we would, we saw nothing but streaming eyes, and faces bathed in tears: and heard nothing but groans and strong cries after God and the Lord Jesus Christ."[72]

But the time would fail me to tell of John Wesley, William Grimshaw, Freeborn Garrettson, Benjamin Abbott, and a whole host of *ignorant and unlearned* Methodist circuit riders; of Daniel Rowlands, Rowland Hill, Lorenzo Dow, Charles G. Finney, Asahel Nettleton, D. L. Moody, A. B. Earle, C. H. Spurgeon, R. A. Torrey, Jonathan Goforth, and Gipsy Smith. Whatever may have been the differences between these men in other respects, this they had in common: they moved their hearers to tears.

People may weep for various reasons, but at the bottom of all reasons lies this fact: the springs of emotion have been opened in their souls.

They are moved—and here is one of the first effects of good preaching. If people are not moved (though it be not necessarily to the point of tears), no good will be accomplished.

Further, good preaching *awakens people*. It rouses them up from carelessness and apathy. It brings them face-to-face with the great realities of life and death and eternity, of God and heaven and hell, of the uncertainty of life and the certainty of judgment.

They likely knew these things before, but they did not think about them. Now they can scarcely think about anything else.

They knew these things before, but now they feel them—as a sword piercing their very soul. They see the flames of hell ever before them. The words are constantly ringing in their ears, "Depart from me, ye cursed, into everlasting fire." They tremble. They determine in good earnest to flee from the wrath to come.

Whereas before they could think of nothing but striving to get ahead in this world, now they can think of nothing but striving to enter in at the strait gate.

But I proceed too fast, and too far. For there is no man upon earth for whom the devil is so mindful of as he is for an awakened sinner. He will do all that he can to take away the seed from their hearts—so it bears no fruit. And he often succeeds.

Nevertheless, though the cares and pleasures of life may often choke out the word—so that a person's serious impressions wear off without resulting in his conversion—those impressions were real while they lasted. He really was awakened to the awful realities of eternity.

And this is an essential characteristic of good preaching: it awakens people. Again and again whole communities have been awakened to the great realities of eternity by the preaching of some man of God. The things of earth, which had so lately engrossed all of their energies, became only trivial and annoying—and the mind of the whole populace became engaged upon the one great concern of religion.

The preaching of George Whitefield was the main element which produced "the great awakening" in England, America, and Scotland. Of the state of things in America in 1740 we read, "The alteration in the face of religion here is altogether surprising. Never did the people show so great a willingness to attend sermons, nor the preachers greater zeal and diligence in performing the duties of their function. Religion is become the subject of most conversations. No books are in request but those of piety and devotion; and instead of idle songs and ballads, the people are everywhere entertaining themselves with psalms and hymns and spiritual songs. All which, under God, is owing to the successful labors of the Rev. Mr. Whitefield."[73]

Under the preaching of Asahel Nettleton, "The interest became so intense in every part of the town, that whenever Mr. Nettleton was seen to enter a house, almost the whole neighborhood would immediately assemble to hear from his lips the Word of life. Husbandmen would leave their fields, mechanics their shops, and females their domestic concerns, to inquire the way to eternal life. Religion was the great and all-absorbing theme in almost all companies, and on almost all occasions."[74]

Of A. B. Earle we read, "Soon converts began to be multiplied, and many were amazed and in doubt, saying one to another, 'What meaneth this?' Instead of the war [the Civil War, in 1863] and the condition of the country, which had been so long the all-engrossing theme, religion became the subject of conversation at the corners of the streets, the marts of business, and in the workshops and mills. All classes and all ages were alike moved, from the little schoolchild to those who had grown gray in the service of Satan."[75]

Francis Asbury says, "The multitudes that attended on this occasion, returning home all alive to God, spread the flame through their respective neighborhoods, which ran from family to family: so that within four weeks several hundreds found peace with God.

"And scarce any conversation was to be heard throughout the circuit, but concerning the things of God: either the complainings of the prisoners, groaning under the spirit of bondage unto fear; or the rejoicing of those whom the Spirit of adoption taught to cry, 'Abba Father!'

"The unhappy disputes between England and her colonies, which just before had engrossed all our conversation [this was written in the Spring of 1776], seemed now in most companies to be forgot, while things of far greater importance lay so near to the heart."[76]

Of the preaching of James Haldane in Scotland we read, "The attention of almost every one was drawn to what they called this *gospel*. It was indeed new to most that heard it, both as to the matter and the manner of delivering it. So generally was the attention of people drawn to it, that you could hardly find two conversing together but religion was the subject."[77] Not only do we often see whole communities thus awakened, but we often see individuals so powerfully awakened that they are quite overcome. They tremble. They cry aloud. They fall senseless to the earth. The apostle John, when brought face-to-face with the Judge of the churches, "fell at his feet as dead." (Rev. 1:17)

Times without number the same has happened when sinners have been brought face-to-face with the Judge of all the earth, under the great preachers of the past. John Nelson relates, "When Mr. Charles Wesley came back from Newcastle, the Lord was with him in such a manner that the pillars of hell seemed to tremble; many that were famous for supporting the devil's kingdom fell to the ground while he was preaching, as if they had been thunderstruck."[78]

Freeborn Garrettson writes, "About forty people gathered; and while I was speaking, the power of the Lord came down in a wonderful manner: nearly half the poor sinners that were present were struck to the floor and cried for mercy, to such a degree that they were heard at a great distance."[79]

Charles G. Finney writes, "I have found myself surrounded by anxious sinners, in such distress as to make every nerve tremble, some overcome with emotion and lying on the floor, some applying camphor to prevent their fainting, others shrieking out as if they were just going to hell."[80]

Oh, that the realities of eternity might once take such hold upon the hearts of sinners in this our day!

Good Preaching Convicts Men of Sin

Further, good preaching *convicts men of sin*. This, though closely related to awakening, is yet a step beyond it. An awakened man may feel himself to be in danger of hellfire; a convicted man feels himself to be deserving of it. An awakened man may be *afraid*; a convicted man is *ashamed*.

Charles G. Finney writes, "Great evils have arisen, and many false hopes have been created by not discriminating between an awakened and a convicted sinner."[81]

It is an easy thing, comparatively, to awaken men, for this is a matter which is primarily concerned with their own good—and they are easily brought to feel that. But *conviction of sin* is concerned primarily with the glory of God, and they care nothing for that. A man may be greatly afraid of the torments of hell, and still believe that God would be most unjust to send him there. Such a one is not convicted of sin, though he is awakened.

We read that the common people and publicans "justified God," while the Pharisees "rejected the counsel of God against themselves." (Luke 7:29-30) A man who is convicted of sin justifies God, while he condemns *himself.*

This is probably the most important of all things. A man cannot be converted while he justifies himself, excuses his sin, and thinks hardly of the just judgment of God. He may—through fear of hell—submit outwardly to the requirements of God, but he does not submit in heart.

He can have neither faith in (nor love for) a God whom he regards as *unjust.*

Charles G. Finney says further, "The fact is, conscience does always condemn the sinner and justify God . . . The real controversy, therefore, is not between God and the conscience, but *between God and the heart* . . . It is for the heart to come over to the ground occupied by the conscience, and thoroughly acquiesce in it as right and true.

"Conscience has a long time been speaking; it has always held one doctrine, and has long been resisted by the heart. Now in conversion, the heart comes over, and gives its full assent to the decisions of conscience; that God is right, and that sin, and himself a sinner, are utterly wrong."[82]

A convicted man is brought to feel guilt—the criminality, offensiveness, and inexcusableness of his sin. He sees the exceeding *sinfulness of sin,* and feels and acknowledges that his way is wicked. Good preaching produces such conviction of sin. Those multitudes whom we have mentioned above, who accepted the counsel of God against themselves (by the mouth of John the Baptist), and justified God, "were all baptized of him in the river of Jordan, confessing their sins." (Mark 1:5)

One of the most marked characteristics of the great Manchurian revivals, under the preaching of Jonathan Goforth, was the same spontaneous, public, humiliating, heart-broken confession of sin. Goforth did not solicit these confessions, but merely preached the Word of God until the people were so convicted of sin that they could not hold their peace. They must speak or burst.

Under the preaching of Freeborn Garrettson, "A man noted for wickedness came cursing and swearing, as he has since told me, but under the first head of the discourse his sins fell, as it were, with the weight of a mill stone on him. 'I would,' said he, 'have run out; but I was afraid to put one foot before the other, lest I should drop into hell, for the pit was disclosed to my view; and I saw no way to escape it; I thought every minute I should fall; but I held myself up by the chair.'"[83]

Under Benjamin Abbott's preaching: "Another instance was a Quaker woman who went from preaching under strong conviction and such anguish of mind that she paid no attention to her family, nor even to her sucking child. Early in the morning I was sent for: when I arrived, she was sitting with both hands clenched fast in the hair of her head, crying out, 'Lord, have mercy on me! Save, Lord, or I perish! I shall go to hell!'"[84]

But now whole generations live and die without ever seeing such things.

Good Preaching Converts People

Further, good preaching *converts people*. It moves them not only to confess their sins, but to forsake them. It moves them to forsake the world, to submit to God, and to join themselves to His people.

Scripture tells us, "The Lord added to the church daily such as should be saved." (Acts 2:47)

William Bramwell wrote, "We have blessed seasons every day, and some are daily saved."[85] And this was in fact true under the ministry of very many of the class to which Bramwell belonged: the most fruitful of all preachers, the early Methodists. We observe in the Scripture quoted that these converts were *added to the church*. That is, they were not of the sort who make a glib profession (based upon an easy and emasculated gospel) and are scarcely seen or heard of again.

Real converts are added to the church. The apostolic churches "increased in number daily." (Acts 16:5) But the churches of today have fallen so far below this standard that they have ceased long ago even to hope or dream of such a thing. Yet nothing short of this is the standard of God's Word, and nothing short of this ought to satisfy us.

Good preaching will produce real converts, and so increase the church in number. There is no truer test of good preaching than this.

We must remark here that when a convert is "added to the church," this cannot mean merely that his name is *added to the membership roll*. There are a great many churches in the land which boast very large membership rolls, and boast also a large number of converts. But when we examine the actual records of these churches, we must say surely there is reason here to be shamed, and not elated. In the first place, of the thousands, or tens of thousands, of converts which are claimed every year, only a small portion are baptized or added to the membership roll. This is bad enough, but what is worse is that among those whose names are added to the membership roll, there are thousands and tens of thousands who do not so much as attend the Sunday morning meetings.

The largest of these churches, which boasts a membership of 67,000, has an average attendance of only 18,000. Now the plain fact is, there are thousands of these members who are not added to the church at all. They are added in name only, but not in fact. They are not "as living stones, built up a spiritual house." They are not living stones. They are not converted. They are not *saved*. The Lord adds to the church *such as are saved*.

Good Preaching Edifies the Church

Finally, good preaching *edifies the church*. This is the business of all preachers, including evangelists. For Scripture says, "He gave some apostles, and some prophets, and some evangelists, and some pastors and teachers, for the perfecting of the saints for the work of the ministry, for the edification of the body of Christ." (Eph. 4:11-12)

Saints are to be edified, that they may engage in the work of the ministry. Edification makes them soul-winners. Acts 9:31 tells us that the churches were edified and (walking in the fear of the Lord and the comfort of the Holy Ghost) were multiplied.

Multiplication follows edification. Thus we are brought again to the fact that the final result of good preaching will be *an increase in number*. Acts 16:5 says, "And so were the churches established in the faith, and increased in number."

An increase in faith will lead directly to an increase in number. This must remain the truest test of good preaching.

Such are the positive effects of good preaching. But there is *another side*.

Good Preaching Divides People

Good preaching *divides people*. "I am come," said Christ, "to set a man at variance against his father, and the daughter against her mother, and the daughter in law against her mother in law. And a man's foes shall be they of his own household." (Matt. 10:35-36) When he preached, "there was a division among the people because of him." (John 7:43)

I have sometimes heard it said that certain doctrines or preachers could not be of God—because they divide churches. It may be so if they divide *godly and holy churches*. But the real fact is, there are fundamental churches all over this land which desperately need to be divided!

They are a mixture of holy and unholy, clean and unclean, saved and lost. Good preaching will divide them in a hurry! It will fill the true saints with joy and blessedness. They will pluck out their eyes and lay down their lives for such a preacher. But it will provoke the enmity, anger, and rage of the ungodly—especially of the *unconverted members* of the church.

And the more scriptural, the more searching, the more powerful a man's preaching is, the more surely it will evoke the enmity of the ungodly.

George Whitefield awakened and converted thousands of sinners, but all the while he was the theme of drunkards' songs, the butt of unclean jests, and the object of cartoons and ribald magazine articles. So were John Wesley and C. H. Spurgeon.

But alas, we have another sort of preacher today—a generation of preachers who offend nobody, please everybody, and do no good to anybody. Such *toothless preaching* is not the work of God's Spirit.

Good preaching divides people.

But why is good preaching so rare? Clearly there is something radically wrong. Most of the fault lies in the shallow and lukewarm state of the church—a state which generally pervades the preachers as well as the people. But there is something further than this: there are many holy, faithful, and devoted men, who yet lack the power of God. They are as David in Saul's armor.

Good Preachers Are Made by God

There is something radically, constitutionally wrong with the way men are *prepared* for the ministry. Men try to make preachers by education and ordination, and the preachers *thus made* lack the first qualifications of a minister of Christ.

John Angell James says, "Incompetent ministers are the burden, as inconsistent ones have been the dishonor of every section of the church, and the hindrance of the progress of the gospel in the world. In hearing many of them, one is ready to wonder how it ever entered into their hearts to conceive they had had been called of God to a work for which they seemed to possess scarcely a single qualification beyond their piety."[86]

Charles G. Finney says, "It is a fact, over which the church is groaning, that the piety of young men suffers so much in the course of their education, that when they enter the ministry, however much intellectual furniture they may posses, they are in a state of spiritual babyhood. They want nursing, and need rather to be fed, than to undertake to feed the church of God."[87]

Further, "I have good reason to know that the churches in many places are deeply pained by the want of living piety and growth in their ministers. Their ministers are intellectual, literary, philosophical, theological in their teaching, but they are sadly deficient in *unction*. They have but little power with God or with man. They instruct the intellect to a certain extent, but they do not meet the wants of the heart. Converts starve under their preaching. They preach an intellectual, rather than a spiritual Gospel."[88]

This is the very truth! The schools of men make ready scribes and learned rabbis, but they *do not make men of God*. God, for the most part, does not do His work by scribes and rabbis, but by *prophets*. And God does not make prophets in the schools of men, but in the wilderness.

John the Baptist "was in the deserts till the day of his shewing unto Israel." (Luke 1:80) Moses, though learned in all the wisdom of the Egyptians, though a man mighty in word and deed, and though called of God for the work, must yet go the back side of the desert for forty years; whence he emerged, like John the Baptist, a prophet of God.

THIS IS THE GREAT NEED OF THE CHURCH TODAY!

We do not want reverends and doctors, but PROPH-ETS. We do not want the wisdom of men, but the *power of God.* We do not want men equipped with the carnal weaponry of rhetoric and elocution, but men mighty through God to the pulling down of strong-holds! We do not want men who are educated in "the wisdom of words" and "excellency of speech," but men who speak with *tongues of fire!*

All of the ministerial schools in the world cannot pro-duce them. If they could, we would have a great abundance of them. What made the early Methodist preachers such a power for God? The great majority of them were—like the apostles—"ignorant and unlearned men."

They had no *ministerial* schools.

Peter Cartwright says, "Suppose, now, Mr. Wesley had been obliged to wait for a literary and theologi-cally-trained band of preachers before he moved in

the glorious work of his day, what would Methodism have been in the Wesleyan connection to-day?
Suppose the Methodist Episcopal Church in these
United States had been under the necessity of waiting for men thus qualified, what would her condition
have been at this time?

"In despite of all of John Wesley's prejudices, he
providentially saw that, to accomplish the glorious
work for which God had raised him up, he must
yield to the superior wisdom of Jehovah, and send
out his 'lay preachers' to wake up a slumbering
world. If Bishop Asbury had waited for their choice
literary band of preachers, infidelity would have
swept these United States from one end to the
other."[89]

Concerning American Methodism he says, "in about
sixty years, more than a million members had been
raised up and united in Church fellowship in the
Methodist Episcopal Church; and this, too, by a body
of uneducated ministers. Perhaps, among the thousands of traveling and local preachers employed and
engaged in this glorious work of saving souls, and
building up the Methodist Church, there were not
fifty men that had any thing more than a common
English education, and scores of them not that; and
not one of them was ever trained in a theological
school or Biblical institute."[90]

Scores and hundreds there were of these pioneer Methodist preachers, who are now long since forgotten. They were "ignorant and unlearned men," who left no writings and had no biographers. But while they lived, they carried the power of God and the fires of revival wherever they went.

Of one such we are told, "He became the living embodiment of his theme, and with a soul on fire he poured out the living truth till every heart was moved. Often have we seen thousands borne down by his impassioned eloquence, like the trees of the forest in a storm. And it was irresistible. Steel your heart as you might; summon all your philosophy and stoicism; and nerve up your soul to an iron insensibility and endurance, surrounding it with a rampart of the strongest prejudice, the lightning of his eloquence accompanied by the deep-toned, awfully-sublime thunder of his words, which came burning from his soul, would melt down your hardness, and break away every fortification in which you were intrenched, while tears from the deep, unsealed fountains of your soul would come unbidden, like the rain. The only way to escape his power was to flee from his presence and hearing."[91]

Next to the early Methodists, perhaps no body of preachers so consistently exhibited the fruits of good preaching as the early Cumberland Presbyterians.

Here was a denomination born of a revival! Awakened souls everywhere were crying for the bread of life.

The harvest was indeed great, but the laborers were few. The scribes and rabbis of the Presbyterian Church could not abide the preaching of uneducated men. Yet there were a few among them who cared more for souls, than they did for a dubious propriety; and though sharing the prejudices of the rest against an "uneducated ministry," they ventured to employ unlearned men who were evidently gifted of God in the ministry of the world.

The opposition continued, and eventually, after trying for some time to put the new wine into the old bottles, they were driven out, and formed the Cumberland Presbyterian Church. Prejudiced as they all were for "ministerial education," they were impelled by the crying need, and indeed forced by necessity (for the new denomination had no schools), to employ an "uneducated ministry."

To satisfy their prejudices as best they might, they prescribed a course of study, and the young men read their books as they rode their horses from one preaching place to another. Meanwhile, they carried the power of God wherever they went. They refused to go into the large cities where there were already established churches, but continually pushed west-ward into the new frontiers. They followed the tide of emigration—to preach the gospel where it was most needed.

"What heroism it required to enter the ministry under our first presbytery! There were no pastorates, no salaries, no possibility of earthly honors. To travel unpaid on horseback across wild wastes to the homes of pioneers in the new settlements; to swim rivers, and sleep on the bare ground; to go hungry and half clad; to belong to a struggling little church whose doctrines and practices were diligently mis-represented, as they are even to this day; to preach in floorless log-cabins, or gather the rough frontiers-men in camps around some spring, and there labor day and night for a week—that poor lost men might be saved, and that our new territories might not all be given over to infidelity; and after all this, to die in poverty at last—was the prospect before that genera-tion of our preachers."[92]

Of one of those preachers we read, "[Philip] McDon-nold was an extemporaneous orator and left no writ-ings at all. The old people said that when he came from the woods (which was the closet of prayer in those days) and went into the pulpit, he was often as white as a sheet. When he began his sermon, pouring down torrents of oratory and fire upon them, there was but one way to resist, and that was to run as quick as possible out of hearing. Wonderful things are related about the effects of his oratory. People said he often made them feel as if the day of judgment had already come."[93] Oh, beloved, this is the kind of preachers and preaching we want! *Nothing less will do.* Myriads of sinners crowd the earth around us—careless, secure, unconcerned—though they are dropping daily and hourly into everlasting flames; and our poor, dull, half-hearted, dry-eyed preaching cannot awaken them, cannot arrest them, cannot convert them. Oh, how we need a baptism of the Holy ghost and of fire! How we need a baptism of tears! But the schools of men cannot give it.

Nay, so far as they affect the matter at all, they stand in the way of our receiving it. The schools of men aim primarily at preparing the mind. God prepares the heart "in the wilderness," in the backside of the desert, or in some unknown nook or corner of the earth, far off from the crowded ways of life. Unseen and unknown by the eyes of men—far way from the centers of learning and culture—God prepares the heart of His prophet. Away on the hillside, following a few sheep in the wilderness, God prepares "a man after His own heart" to shepherd His people Israel.

The mind may be cultured or uncultured, educated or uneducated. God can use the learned and cultured

John Wesley, or the ignorant and uncouth Bud Robinson. He can use the college-bred George Whitefield, or the field-born Gipsy Smith, who never went to school for one day in his life.

He can use the fine diction and elocution of Charles G. Finney, or the blundering grammar and mispronounced words of D. L. Moody. Indeed, I have no doubt that God prefers to use the weak and the base and the despised; and the majority of the greatest preachers have been ignorant and unlearned men, even as were the apostles of Christ, Paul excepted. Yet God can use the learned also, where the heart and spirit are right.

The education, or lack of it, no more makes the preacher than the saddle makes the horse. We are often told that men must be educated in order to reach the educated. But the doctrines of the Bible are directly against such reasoning, and so are the facts of history. Of D. L. Moody (who could scarcely read when he began his work) we read, "One day during his great mission in London, Mr. Moody was holding a meeting in a theatre packed with a most select audience. Noblemen and noblewomen were there in large numbers. A prominent member of the royal family was in the royal box. Mr. Moody arose to read the Scripture lesson. He attempted to read Luke 4:27: 'And many lepers were in Israel in the time of Eliseus the prophet.' When he came to the name *Eliseus*, he stammered and stuttered over it. He went back to the beginning of the verse and began to read again, but again when he reached the word 'Eliseus' he could not get over it. He went back and began the third time to read the verse but again the word "Eliseus" was too much for him.

"He closed the Bible with deep emotion and looked up and said, 'Oh, God! Use this stammering tongue to preach Christ crucified to these people.' The power of God came upon him and one who heard him often at other times said to me afterwards that he had never heard Mr. Moody pour out his soul in such a torrent of eloquence as he did then, and the whole audience was melted by the power of God."[94]

Many such examples might be related, but I confine myself to the following: "George W., a strong Cincinnati lawyer, attended a revival meeting held by Rev. H. Haynes, a friend of mine, for the avowed purpose of showing up the fallacy of revealed religion, but before the meeting closed George was powerfully converted to God.

"Bro. Haynes had fired his gospel gun at him a number of times, and thought that he had hit him." All were desirous to know the instrumentality God had used in his conversion. "There was at the meeting a man called 'Bud Thomas,' who was but one remove above an idiot, but was very pious, and lived around among the people.

"George, in relating the circumstances of his awakening, said, 'I attended this meeting several days as a confirmed infidel, but at the love- feast when I heard Bud Thomas talk with so much clearness and confidence about his mother in heaven, and how she used to pray for her poor, afflicted boy, and how much he loved Jesus, and of his bright hopes of meeting his dear mother in heaven, I wept. I wept, and I saw in his simple experience the truth and beauty of religion with such clearness that my infidelity went like the mist of the morning before the rising sun."[95] Yet such was the prejudice of the author who relates this example, that on the very next page he tell us that "literary education is all-important"!

The Secret is in the Heart

The great qualifications of a good preacher do not lie primarily in his head at all, but in his *heart*. The great Gipsy Smith says, "I was preaching one night in a great western city. At the close of the service, a dear old minister came into the ante-room, where I sat alone. He had his day, this white-haired, saintly brother, and was waiting for his Lord. He came into the room and walked straight up to me and put his hand upon my head. I thought he was going to bless me, and stood for a moment with closed eyes, waiting for the prophet's blessing. I thought he was going to bless me, or to pray for me, but instead he began to feel my head. Then I became curious and said, 'Are you a phrenologist, or what is the trouble?'

"He replied, 'I am trying to find out the secret of your success.'

"I said, 'You are feeling too high. Come down here' (indicating the position of my heart). 'It is not in the head. It is in the heart that the secret lies!'"[96]

We shall have more to say, further on, of the great heart of this great man. Meanwhile, we may smile at the foolish ignorance of the old minister who thought to discover the secret of his power by feeling his head. But we can not smile at the foolish ignorance of the ministerial schools which think to make preachers by educating their heads. Over that ignorance we can only weep.

The secret lies, indeed, in the heart. What sort of heart, then, must a man have in order to be a good preacher? Without pretending to say all that might be said on the subject, we affirm that he must have a *full heart, a burning heart, and a broken heart.*

A Full Heart

A *full heart*. Observe, we do not say a full mind. There is a vast difference. A man may have his mind filled with the truth, and it yet do no good to himself or anyone else. He may hold the truth in sectarian bigotry. He may hold the truth in unrighteousness. He may hold the truth, and not walk in it.

But if the truth *holds him*, it is truth in the heart. Then he walks in it. Then the savor of it fills his whole life. For out of the heart are the issues of life. (Prov.4:23)

When Elijah was to be translated, the sons of the prophets had the same knowledge of it that Elisha had; but they had it in the mind: Elisha had it in the heart. They could all say to Elisha, "Knowest thou that the Lord will take away thy master from thy head today?" But their knowledge had no effect upon them. They knew that the great prophet was to be taken away that day, but they cared not. They cared not enough to follow him to see the matter come to pass. It was altogether different with Elisha. He had but one word on his tongue: "As the Lord liveth, and as thy soul liveth, I will not leave thee." He knew no more than the sons of the prophets, but he cared more. They had the truth in their heads, he in his heart. They were theological students; Elisha was a prophet.

But in speaking as we have done of ministerial education, we do not mean in any way to countenance or condone *ignorance*. We value knowledge, provided it be the right kind of knowledge, held *in the right way*.

A mind full of psychology and rhetoric, and of "the arts and science," we do indeed account to be of little worth. But a heart filled with the things of God we account to be of the greatest worth and importance. But the schools cannot give it. We might indeed get the letter of Scripture *in the head* by going to school. But to get the spirit and power of it *in the heart* is quite another thing. And this is what we mean by a full heart.

We have observed above that a man may be very useful, if he is earnest and fervent, though he be very limited in knowledge. And this is true, but it has its limitations.

Writing (in 1869) of the great awakening which swept through Ireland in 1859, C. H. Mackintosh says, "At the commencement of this movement we observe a class of men who took a prominent place in the work, earnest men, we doubt not, who having been recently converted to Christ, and being filled with a deep sense of the value of immortal souls, sought to press upon others the one or two points of truth of which they themselves had got hold. These men, however they might have been, and assuredly were, used of God, have not proved efficient instruments in the important work of building up souls. They filled a place, at a moment when the Spirit of God was striking down; but they do not appear to be available now that he is building up."[97] Such a man was Paul at his conversion. He immediately preached with power to the confounding of the Jews. Yet his preaching must have been very limited in scope, and after this he must again pass into obscurity in Arabia and in Tarsus, to emerge again some years later with a full heart, the possessor of "abundance of revelations."

"For out of the abundance of the heart the mouth speaketh. A good man out of the good treasure of the heart bringeth forth good things." (Matt. 12:34-35)

Here is the first reason for the success and power of the great preachers of the past: they had full hearts, and out of that fullness their mouths spoke. They did not sit down with "pulpit commentaries" and books of sermon outlines and sermon illustrations to make out a sermon on paper, to carry with them into the pulpit. There was no need of this, for out of their bellies flowed rivers of living water. Their hearts were full, and it was impossible that they should stand before a congregation of perishing sinners and be at any loss for what to say.

Of this John Newton says, "I believe, my dear friends, if our minds were duly impressed with all the topics of the gospel, it would be difficult to study a sermon. If I was sure that both I and all my auditory were to die and appear before God the moment I had finished my next sermon, how little should I attend to the minutiae of arrangement and style! My heart would teach my mouth, my thoughts would be weighty, too big indeed for words fully to express; yet it is probable they would find the fittest words I was master of, waiting for employment."[98] He testifies further, "And so far as I can judge of myself, I seldom succeed better than when hurry and engagements constrain me to speak without five minutes premeditation; sometimes without being determined as to my text five minutes before I go into the pulpit."[99] I do not regard Newton as one of the greatest of preachers, for his manner may not have been equal to his matter; yet he was a good and *fruitful* preacher, and—the abundance of his heart teaching his mouth— he had no need to prepare sermons.

It has been mentioned above that George Whitefield, one of the greatest of preachers, did not prepare sermons. Indeed, he says, "The best preparation for preaching on Sundays, is to preach every day in the week."[100]

He did preach every day in the week, usually twice a day, and often for two hours at a time. And all of this without preparing sermons—for out of the abundance of his heart, his mouth spoke. Hear him as he stands before a congregation of perishing sinners: "Many such reflections as these, my brethren, crowd in upon my mind. At present, blessed be the Lord, who delights to magnify His strength in a poor worm's weakness, I am at a stand, not so much about what I shall say, as what I shall leave *unsaid*. My belly, like Elihu's, is, as it were, full of new wine; 'out of the abundance of my heart my mouth speaketh.' The seeing so great a multitude standing before me; a sense of the infinite majesty of that God in whose name I preach, and before whom I, as well as you, appear to give an account; and the uncertainty there is whether I shall live another day to speak to you any more: these considerations, especially the presence of God which I now feel upon my soul, furnishes me with so much matter, that I scarce know where to begin or where to end my application."[101]

Neither did Whitefield weary his hearers, as must be evident by the fact that thousands of them flocked to hear him day after day for thirty years. Those who weary their hearers are those who preach second-hand truth from commentaries and illustration books.

Of Howell Harris we read, "He began to speak hundreds of times without having any idea as to what he was going to say. He would go on thus, pouring out old things and new for two, three, or even four hours. Indeed. We have instances of his services continuing without a break for six hours."[102]

So successful was his preaching that, having started from nothing in 1736, by 1739 he had organized hundreds of converts into about thirty societies.

Of Gipsy Smith we read, "He never knows until he enters the pulpit, unless his 'life story' has been announced, what his subject will be. Often in the vestry he will say, 'What am I to do tonight? He watches his congregation, tries to diagnose the situation, and very often, even if he has used a text, finds himself suddenly led into a discourse which he had not thought of."[103]

Charles G. Finney says, "When I first began to preach, and for some twelve years of my earliest ministry, I wrote not a word; and was most commonly obliged to preach without any preparation whatever, except what I got in prayer. Oftentimes I went into the pulpit without knowing upon what text I should speak, or a word that I should say. I depended on the occasion and the Holy Spirit to suggest the text, and to open up the whole subject to my mind; and certainly in no part of my ministry have I preached with greater success and power."[104]

I forbear saying any more on this subject, though a book could be written on this alone. It is evident that these men preached from *full hearts*. I think it is evident also that much of the preaching in the church today is not from full hearts; indeed, much of it is not from the heart at all. It may be truth, but it is not truth written in the preacher's heart by the finger of God — it is the letter of truth, without the spirit and power of it; truth known in the mind, but little felt in the heart, and dealt out cold and dry and powerless.

It does not come gushing fresh and warm from a full heart, and therefore it does not do its work.

A Burning Heart

This is closely related to the last point, yet distinct. A *burning heart* is a heart which is not only full of the truth, but which is on fire with it. It is a fervent heart, a heart which feels the truth it handles.

It is my conviction that more depends upon this than upon all besides—that the degree in which a man possesses a burning heart will go farther than any other thing to determine his power, or lack of it. It is *fervent preaching* that is powerful. It is a burning heart that makes preaching fervent.

Of John the Baptist, perhaps the greatest man and greatest preacher who ever walked the earth, we read, "He was a burning and shining light . . ." (John 5:35) A light that does not burn is no light at all. And what burns, if not the heart?

Those who listened to Christ expound the Scripture said, "Did not our heart burn within us while he talked with us by the way?" (Luke 24:32)

Among all of the great preachers whom we could mention, perhaps we could find no better example of a burning heart than in Gipsy Smith. Harold Murray says, "When first I watched him in his meetings and saw the tears running down his own cheeks as he told a story that brought tears to the eyes of his hearers, I wondered. It could not be superb acting. No, it was not. The time came when I saw him behaving in exactly the same way when there was no crowd. I saw him weep, when practically alone, in the forest where he was born; in the lane where his mother died. He can no more keep back the tears when he thinks of the past, of those he has loved, of the dying boys to whom he ministered in France, than he could stem the Atlantic ocean."[105]

Gipsy Smith felt things, and hence he made others feel them."He has won them not by brilliance and skill in theological argument but just by being himself and communicating his own depth of feeling."[106]

Of John Fletcher we are told, "Prayer, praise, love, and zeal, all ardent, elevated above what one would think attainable in this state of frailty, were the element in which he continually lived. And as to others, his one employment was to call, entreat, and urge them to ascend with him to the glorious Source of being and blessedness. He had leisure comparatively for nothing else. Languages, arts, sciences, grammar, rhetoric, logic, even divinity itself, as it is called, were all laid aside when he appeared in the school room among the students. His full heart would not suffer him to be silent. He must speak, and they were readier to hearken to this servant and minister of Jesus Christ than to attend to Sal-lust, Virgil, Cicero, or any Latin or Greek historian, poet, or philosopher they had been engaged in reading. And they seldom hearkened long, before they were all in tears, and every heart [caught] fire from the flame that burned in his soul."[107]

Here we have the proper method of communicating truth. We must burn it into the people's hearts. And in order to do that, we must have a burning heart ourselves. "Homiletics" prescribes a certain organization and arrangement of our material, in order that people may remember it. But it will not work. Let anyone who follows these methods put it to the test upon his own hearers, and see what they remember of his sermons after the lapse of but one week. He will likely be greatly humiliated at the result.

But truth which is *burned into the heart* cannot be forgotten.

It is not a neatly arranged pile of sticks which will warm people, but *fire*. It is not a neatly arranged pile of doctrines, or points, or divisions and subdivisions, that will warm hearts, but fire. There is no order or arrangement under the sun which will accomplish the work of God in the souls of men. What we want is the baptism of the Holy Ghost and fire.

What we want is a burning heart.

C. H. Spurgeon says, "I do not believe that God the Holy Ghost cares one single atom about your classical composition. I do not think that the Lord takes any delight in your rhetoric, or in your poetry, or even in that marvelous peroration which concludes the discourse, after the manner of the final display at old Vauxhall Gardens, when a profusion of all manner of fireworks closed the scene. Not even by that magnificent finale does the Lord work the salvation of sinners. If there is fire, life, and truth in the sermon, then the quickening Spirit will work by it, but not else. Be earnest and you need not be elegant."[108]

Elsewhere he says, "It is dreadful work to listen to a sermon and feel all the while as if you were sitting out in a snowstorm, or dwelling in a house of ice, clear but cold, orderly but killing. You have said to yourself, 'That was a well-divided and well-planned sermon, but I cannot make out what was the matter with it;' the secret being that there was the wood, but no fire to kindle it . . . We prefer a sermon in which there may be no vast talent, and no great depth of thought; but what there is has come fresh from the crucible, and, like molten metal, burns its way."[109]

We have referred earlier to the young man who heard George Whitefield, and afterwards, for days and weeks together, could scarcely think of anything but: "The wrath's to come! The wrath's to come!" It was not psychology or rhetoric that produced this, but the burning heart and the flood of tears.

Another writes, "In September 1741, I went to hear Mr. Whitefield in Glasgow. Some of his first sermons renewed my concern for a time; but those he delivered on the Tuesday, just before leaving, melted my heart."[110] Do homiletical arrangements melt hearts? Do alliterated outlines melt hearts? This is not the fruit of any homiletical principles whatsoever, but of a burning heart—of a tongue of fire, speaking out of the abundance of a burning heart.

As for remembering sermons, Thomas Rankin says of the first time he heard Whitefield preach, "I remembered more of that sermon than of all the sermons I had ever heard."[111]

But I must add further observation on this point: it is not the purpose of preaching merely to fill the mind with truths, but rather to move the heart—to bring the soul into the spirit and power of those truths. It is of little merit whether the letter of our sermons is remembered, if permanent good is wrought by them in the hearts of the hearers, if souls are saved, if saints are brought into the spirit and power of the truth. Of Whitefield's sermons Cornelius Winter writes, "Though I have lost much of the letter of his sermon, the savor of them yet remains."[112]

Peter Cartwright relates a similar thing of the preaching of Henry Bascom: "to which," he says, "I yielded myself up as to an elysian dram. A friend behind me every now and then exclaimed, 'O, I am afraid he will quit!' Strange to say, while I remember that discourse as wonderful, I can not call to mind any of it. . . . A friend who said, 'He took my soul out of me, and after shaking it well, put it back, without giving a new idea,' seems to have had a similar experience." [113]

Here, we may suppose, was good preaching, yet in the one case, no new truth communicated, and in the other, the letter of it entirely forgotten. But the *savor of it* was not forgotten. For that was burned into the heart.

Another example of the same thing is found in the effect of Henry Moorhouse's preaching upon D. L. Moody. Moorhouse was an unlearned man who knew nothing of homiletics or rhetoric, but who preached from a full and burning heart. He went to Moody's church in Chicago and preached seven nights in succession from John 3:16. Moody was absent the first two nights. When he returned he asked his wife about the preaching of Moorhouse: "she says, 'I think you will like him, although he preaches a little different from what you do.'

"'How is that?'

"'Well, he tells sinners God loves them.'

"'Well, ' said I, 'he is wrong.'

"She said, 'I think you will agree with him when you hear him, because he backs up every thing he says with the Word of God. You think if a man don't preach as you do he is wrong.'

"I went down that night to church and I noticed every one brought his Bible. 'Now,' he said, 'my friends, if you will turn to the third chapter of John and the sixteenth verse, you will find my text.' He preached a most extraordinary sermon from that sixteenth verse. He did not divide the text into secondly and thirdly and fourthly—he just took the whole text, and then went through the Bible from Genesis to Revelation to prove that in all ages God loved the world; that He sent prophets and patriarchs and holy men to warn us, and sent His Son, and after they murdered Him, He sent the Holy Ghost. I never knew, up to that time, that God loved us so much. This heart of mine began to thaw out, and I could not keep back the tears."[114]

Moody goes on to relate how Moorhouse seemed to strike a higher chord on each succeeding evening, preaching in the same manner, from the same text, until the love of God became a living reality to his hearers.

Now whether or not Moody remembered the letter of these sermons is immaterial. The savor of them never left him. It was burned into his heart. It sent him forth with a new message, with which he was to draw and melt the hearts of thousands. And all of this was done with no homiletical arrangement, and no prepared sermons. It was done by a burning heart.

When will preachers open their eyes to the import of these plain facts?

R. A. Torrey says, "Brethren, that is what we need in the pulpit: ministers on fire. What cold men most of us preachers are! Orthodox enough, it may be, and we present the most solemn truth with great force of reason, and great beauty of rhetoric, and most convincing eloquence; and our audiences sit there and admire our strong preaching, but they do not repent of their sins. Why not? Because we are not on fire. We convince the intellect, but we do not melt the heart. But put a minister who is on fire in the pulpit— Wesley was such a man, Whitefield was such a man; Charles G. Finney was such a man— put a man on fire in the pulpit, and the audience will melt."[115]

A Broken Heart

D. L. Moody's wife states that Moody said "no one had a right to preach hell except with a *broken heart*."[117] The apostle Paul had great heaviness and continual sorrow in his heart for his lost countrymen. Christ wept over them. And, indeed, he who does not, must have a calloused heart. C. H. Spurgeon says, "It is a horrible thing for a man to be so doctrinal that he can speak coolly of the doom of the wicked, so that, if he does not actually praise God for it, it costs him no anguish of heart to think of the ruin of millions of our race. This is horrible! I hate to hear the terrors of the Lord proclaimed by men whose hard visages, harsh tones, and unfeeling spirit betray a sort of doctrinal desiccation: all the milk of human kindness is dried out of them. Having no feeling himself, such a preacher creates none."[116]

D. L. Moody possessed that broken heart, and it was that which gave him what one describes as "that beseeching tenderness of tone I have never heard in anyone else."[118] He was full of tenderness and compassion in all of his dealings with souls. The same writer says of his preaching, "But such pleading!—no words of mine can give a fit idea of it; he seemed to pour out his soul in earnest entreaty, and with tears he besought them all, on this his last night of gospel preaching in Glasgow, to seek the Lord, and they would surely find him."[119]

R. A. Torrey was a man of less emotion. He did not usually weep when he preached. He was not overcome with emotion while he pled with sinners. Yet in spite of his deficiencies in this matter, he melted the hearts of sinners. "Listen to him as he faces a crowd of drunken men and women and tells them of the love of Jesus. No word of reproach falls from his lips. In simple language he speaks of the Savior's love in such a manner that the hardest conscience is awakened and the coldest heart touched. Tenderly does he plead with them to quit sin—so tenderly and lovingly that tears steal down the grimy faces, and miracles of grace are numbered by the hundreds."[120]

How is this to be accounted for? How does a man who does not weep himself make others weep? Beneath his apparently cold exterior lies a *broken heart*. At the Conference on Christian Fundamentals held in Philadelphia in 1919 he said, "The subject assigned to me for this afternoon is *Future Punishment*. I shrink from speaking on that subject. I have a dread that approaches horror of speaking on that subject. I have lain on my face before God and sobbed as I have thought of what the Bible clearly teaches on the subject, and thought also of what it involves. It has seemed to me, time and again, that I could not have it so. I believe I would gladly die in agony and shame if thereby I could make it sure that all men would somewhere, sometime, somehow be brought to repentance and thus [be] saved. To me the doctrine of *Future Punishment* is not a mere matter of speculative theory that I could discuss without emotion in cold intellectuality."[121]

Torrey preached a great deal on hell, the day of judgment, and the wrath of God; but he preached these things out of a broken heart, and therefore the people were softened and melted down while they were convicted, and hundreds of them were converted.

The Unction of the Holy Ghost

We have but one final matter to mention: *the unction of the Holy Ghost*. Without this, our preaching will be barren and unfruitful. I do believe that a man who possesses the qualification of heart mentioned above will, in general, be a man full of the Holy Ghost.

There is nothing mysterious about this. John Fletcher wrote, "An over eager attention to the doctrine of the Spirit has made me, in some degree, overlook the medium by which the Spirit works, I mean the Word of truth, which is the wood by which the heavenly fire warms us. I rather expected lightning than a steady fire by means of fuel."[122] Lighting would please us better, for we are apt to like a quick and easy way. But none such exists. Yet a steady use of the Word of truth—not scholastically, but to walk with God, to perfect holiness, to change hearts, to convert sinners—this, by a man who is devoted heart, soul, mind, and strength to the cause of Christ, is the path to the fullness of the Holy Ghost and the power of God.

Yet it is possible for a man to have the qualification mentioned above, and yet lack the power of the Holy Ghost. Moreover, it is possible for him to have it, and afterwards to lose it, as Samson did. The subject is too large to enter upon here, yet we cannot close without a few words on it. It is very common in our day to be told that we are *not* to seek the baptism of the Holy Spirit, that it has been given to the church once for all, never to be repeated, that it is folly to seek something which we already have, that we are laying ourselves open to the devil's counterfeits, and so forth. Such statements I answer two ways: First, the originators and teachers of such doctrines have not been the great preachers of the church—they have not been the great evangelists, nor the great soul-winners, nor the men with burning hearts and flaming tongues—but merely scholastic preachers of doctrine. The great preachers, as a body, have been on the other side. They have earnestly contended for the indispensable necessity of the baptism of the Holy Ghost—as the foremost qualification for a preacher of the gospel.

C. H. Spurgeon, D. L. Moody, R. A. Torrey, Jonathan Goforth, A. B. Earle, Charles G. Finney, and others have explicitly contended for this doctrine.

In the second place, the apostles were told, "Ye shall receive power after that [or, when] the Holy Ghost is come upon you." (Acts 1:8) "Tarry ye in the city of Jerusalem until ye be endued with power from on high." (Luke 24:49) Now of what possible use can it be for our modern, *scholastic preachers* to argue that they already have the baptism of the Holy Ghost, when it is evident (to the whole world) that they do not have the *power?*

Brethren, we want reality. We want the power of the Holy Ghost. The world goes to hell because we have it not, while we contend about words and names. Call it whatever you wish—call it *the baptism, the unction, the anointing, the filling, the fullness,* or whatever you please—but for God's sake, for Christ's sake, for the sake of perishing sinners, cease to make an empty profession, or an empty doctrine of it, and get on your face before God until you possess it! Then will you know, by your own happy experience, what good preaching is.

Prayer

LEONARD RAVENHILL

Prayer

LEONARD RAVENHILL

*T*here's nothing more transfiguring than prayer. People often ask, "Why do you insist on prayer so much?" The answer is very simple—because Jesus did.

The Gospel of Prayer

You could change the title of *The Gospel According to St. Luke* to *The Gospel of Prayer*. It's the prayer life of Jesus. The other evangelists say that Jesus was in the Jordan and the Spirit descended on Him. The other evangelists say that Jesus chose twelve disciples. Luke says it was after He spent a night in prayer that He chose twelve disciples. The other evangelists say that Jesus died on a cross. Luke says that even when He was dying, Jesus was praying for those who persecuted Him. The other evangelists say Jesus went on a mount and He was transfigured. There's nothing more transfiguring than prayer.

The Scriptures say that the disciples *went to bed*, but Jesus *went to pray*—as was His custom. It was His custom to pray. Now Jesus was the Son of God. He was definitely anointed for His ministry. If Jesus needed all that time in prayer, don't you and I need time in prayer? If Jesus needed it in every crisis, don't you and I need it in every crisis?

The story goes that a group of tourists visiting a picturesque village saw an old man sitting by a fence. In a rather patronizing way, one of the visitors asked, "Were any great men born in this village?" Without looking up the old man replied, "No, only babies."

The greatest men were once babies. The greatest saints were once toddlers in the things of the Spirit. C.H. Spurgeon was converted at the age of sixteen and began preaching in London at the age of nineteen. When he was twenty seven, they built him a tabernacle seating 6,000, which he packed twice on Sundays. That's 12,000 and once on Thursday nights. How? He waited on God. He got alone with God. He studied, and he prayed.

Desperate Prayer

God makes all His best people in loneliness. Do you know what the secret of praying is? *Praying in secret.*

"But you, when you pray, go into your inner room, and
when you have shut your door . . ." (Matt. 6:6)

You can't show off when the door's shut and nobody's there. You can't display your gifts. You can impress others, but you can't impress God.

First Samuel 1:1-15 gives an account of the yearly trip Elkanah and his wife, Hannah, made to Shiloh to worship and sacrifice to the Lord. During this time, Hannah had been distressed that she was not able to bear a son for her husband. This passage of Scripture gives quite a descriptive account of her time in prayer concerning the barrenness of her womb. It says that Hannah wept. More than this, she wept until she was sore. She poured out her soul before the Lord. Her heart was grieving; she was bitter of soul, provoked, and of a sorrowful spirit.

Now that's a pretty good list of afflictions: sorrow, hardship, and everything else that came upon this woman. But the key to the whole situation is that *she was a praying woman*. In verse 20 it says that she reaped her reward:

"And it came about in due time, after Hannah had conceived, that she gave birth to a son; and she named him Samuel, saying, "Because I have asked him of the Lord."

Now I say very often, and people don't like it, that God doesn't answer prayer. He answers *desperate prayer!* Your prayer life denotes how much you depend on your own ability, and how much you really believe in your heart when you sing, "Nothing in my hands I bring, simply to Thy cross I cling." The more self confidence you have, the less you pray. The less self confidence you have, the more you *have to pray.*

What does the Scripture say? It says that God takes the lowly, the things that are not. Paul says in First Corinthians 1:28 that God takes the things that are not to bring to nothing the things that are, so that no flesh should glory in His presence. We need a bunch of "are nots" today.

The Language of the Poor

Prayer is the language of the poor. Over and over again David, the King of Israel, says, *"Incline Thine ear, O Lord, and answer me; for I am afflicted and needy." (Psalm 86:1)* And do you remember that one of the greatest psalms he wrote says, *"This poor man cried and the Lord heard him..." (Psalm 34:6)*

The apostle Paul overwhelms me with his spirituality, his pedigree, and his colossal intellect. Yet he says that he's very conscious that when he's weak, he is strong. He was always trying to prove to himself and to others that he was a *nobody*.

True prayer is a two way communication. I speak to God and God speaks to me. I don't know how the Spirit makes communication, or why God needs me to pray, but that's how God works.

Get Up and Pray!

One day I was at a conference with Dr. Raymond Edmond of Wheaton College, one of the greatest Christian educators in this country. He told us of an experience he had while he was in Uruguay as a missionary. He hadn't been there long before he was sick and dying. He was so near death that they had already dug his grave. He had great beads of sweat on his brow and there was a death-rattle in his throat. But suddenly he sat straight up in bed and said to his wife, "Bring me my clothes!" Nobody knew what had happened.

Many years later he was retelling the story in Boston. Afterward, a little old lady with a small, dog-eared, beaten up book, approached him and asked, "What day did you say you were dying? What time was it in Uruguay? What time would it be in Boston?" When he answered her, her wrinkled face lit up. Pointing to her book, she said, "There it is, you see?

At 2 a.m. God said to get up and pray; the devil's trying to kill Raymond Edmond in Uruguay." And she had gotten up and prayed.

Duncan Campbell told the story of hearing a farmer in his field who was praying. He was praying about Greece. Afterward, he asked him why he was praying. The man said, "I don't know. I had a burden in the spirit and God said, "You pray, there's someone in Greece that is in a bad situation. I prayed until I got a release."

Some time later the farmer was in a meeting listening to a missionary. The man described a time when he was working in Greece. He had been in serious trouble. The time? Two or three years ago. The men compared notes and discovered that it was the very same day that God had burdened a farmer on a little island off the coast of Scotland to pray for a man in Greece—whose name he didn't even know. It may seem the Lord gives you strange things. I don't care. If the Lord tells you something, carry on with what the Lord tells you.

Who Shall Ascend to the Hill of the Lord?

There's another experience Duncan Campbell told about when he was working in Scotland. "I couldn't preach," he said. "I couldn't get through to God. The heavens were solid. It was as though there was a ten foot ceiling of steel." So he quit trying to preach. Instead, he asked a young man named John Cameron to pray. The boy stood up and said, "What's the use of praying if we're not right with God?" He then quoted the 24th Psalm, *"Who may ascend into the hill of the Lord?"*

You can't approach God unless your hands are clean, which means your relationships with others are clean and your heart is clean. *"Who may ascend into the hill of the Lord? He who has clean hands and a pure heart..."* (Psalm 24:3-4)

After the boy recited Psalm 24 he began to pray. He prayed 10, 15, 20 minutes. Then he suddenly said, "Excuse me, Lord, while I resist the devil." He turned around and began to tell the devil where to go and how to get there. He fought for all he was worth. You talk about having on the armor of God and resisting the devil! When he finished resisting the devil, he finished his prayer. He had prayed for forty five minutes! When he finished praying it was as though God had pulled a little switch in heaven. The Spirit of God came down on that church, that community, on the dance hall at the other end of town, and on the tavern at the end of town.

Revival was born in that prayer!

At the end of Malachi it says, *"And the Lord, whom you seek, will suddenly* (that's the word I like, *suddenly*) *come to His Temple." (Malachi 3:1)* Remember what it says about the shepherds? They were watching their flocks by night when *suddenly* there was the sound of the heavenly host. Do you remember a bunch of men who had been waiting in the upper room? *Suddenly* the Holy Spirit came on them in that room.

There's a date in history that I love very much. It was Wednesday, August 13th, 1737. A little group of people in Moravia were waiting in a prayer meeting. At 11:00 *suddenly* the Holy Spirit came. Do you know what happened? The prayer meeting that began at 11:00 lasted one hundred years! That's right. That prayer room was not empty for a century! It's the longest prayer among men and women that I know of. Even children six and seven years old travailed in prayer for countries whose names they couldn't even spell.

Why We Don't Have Revival

In an old town in Ireland they'll show you with reverence a place where four young men met night after night after night praying for revival. In Wales, there's a place in the hills where three or four young men — only eighteen or nineteen years old — met and prayed night after night. They wouldn't let God go; they would not take no for an answer. As far as humanly possible they prayed a revival into birth. If you're thinking of revival at your church without any inconvenience, forget it. Revival costs a lot.

I can give you one simple reason why we don't have revival in America. Because we're content to live without it. We're not seeking *God*, we're seeking *miracles;* we're seeking big crusades; we're seeking blessings. In Numbers 11, Moses said to God, *"You're asking me to carry a burden I can't handle. Do something or kill me!"* Do you love America enough to say, "God, send revival or kill me?" Do you think it's time we changed Patrick Henry's prayer from, "Give me liberty or give me death," to "Give me revival or let me die"?

In the 30th chapter of Genesis, Rachael goes to Jacob and throws herself down in despair. She says, "Give me children or else I die." Are you willing to throw yourself down before God to seek the spiritual birth of spiritual children in our country?

People say, "I'm filled with the Holy Spirit." If the coming of the Spirit didn't revolutionize your prayer life, you'd better check on it. I'm not so sure you got what God wanted you to get. We've said that prayer changes things. No! Prayer doesn't change *things*. Prayer changes *people* and *they* change things. We all want Gabriel to do the job. God says, *"Do it yourself, with My sufficiency and My strength."*

We need to get like this woman, Hannah. What did she do? She wept, she was grieved, and she said she had a complaint; she fasted, and she prayed.

Jesus, the anointed of God, made prayer His custom. Paul with his background and intellect, depended on prayer because he said he was weak. David, the king, called himself a poor man and cried to the Lord. Hannah prayed for a son and gave birth to a prophet. The prayers of a handful of young men sparked revival.

There's nothing more transfiguring than prayer.

Power

E. M. BOUNDS

"The thing far above all other things in the equipment of the preacher is prayer. Before everything else, he must be a man who makes a specialty of prayer.

A prayerless preacher is a misnomer. He has either missed his calling, or has grievously failed God who called him into the ministry. God wants men who are not ignoramuses, but those who "study to show themselves approved." Preaching the Word is essential; social qualities are not to be underestimated, and education is good; but under and above all else, prayer must be the main plank in the platform of the man who goes forth to preach the unsearchable riches of Christ to a lost and hungry world."

—E. M. Bounds

Power Through Prayer

E. M. BOUNDS

*W*e are constantly on a stretch, if not on a strain, to devise new methods, new plans, new organizations to advance the Church and secure enlargement and efficiency for the gospel. This trend of the day has a tendency to lose sight of the man or sink the man in the plan or organization. God's plan is to make much of the man, far more of him than anything else.

Men Are God's Method

The Church is looking for better methods; God is looking for better men. What the church needs today is not more machinery or better, not new organizations or more and novel methods, but men whom the Holy Ghost can use—men of prayer, men mighty in prayer. The Holy Ghost does not flow through methods, but through men. He does not come on machinery, but on men. He does not anoint plans, but men—*men of prayer*.

The man makes the preacher. God must make the man. The messenger is, if possible, more than the message. The preacher is more than the sermon. The preacher makes the sermon. As the life giving milk from the mother's bosom is but the mother's life, so all the preacher says is tinctured, impregnated by what the preacher is. The treasure is in earthen vessels and the taste of the vessel impregnates and may discolor. The man, the whole man, lies behind the sermon. Preaching is not the performance of an hour. It is the outflow of a life. It takes twenty years to make a sermon, because it takes twenty years to make the man. The true sermon is a thing of life. The sermon grows because the man grows. The sermon is forceful because the man is forceful. The sermon is holy because the man is holy. The sermon is full of the divine unction because the man is full of the divine unction.

The sermon cannot rise in its life giving forces above the man. Dead men give out dead sermons, and dead sermons kill. Everything depends upon the spiritual character of the preacher. Under the Jewish dispensation the high priest had inscribed in dual letters on a golden frontlet: *"Holiness unto the Lord."* So every preacher in Christ's ministry must be molded into and mastered by this same holy motto. Jonathan Edwards said: "I went on with my eager pursuit after more holiness and more conformity to Christ. The heaven I desired was the heaven of holiness."

God's Men Have God's Character

The constraining power of love must be in the preacher as a projecting, eccentric, all commanding, self oblivious force.

The energy of self denial must be his being, his heart and blood and bones.

He must go forth as a man among men, clothed with humility, abiding in meekness, wise as a serpent, harmless as a dove; the bonds of a servant with the spirit of a king, a king in high, royal, independent bearing, with the simplicity and sweetness of a child.

The preacher must throw himself, with all the abandon of a perfect, self emptying faith and a self consuming zeal, into his work for the salvation of men. Hearty, heroic, compassionate, fearless martyrs must the men be who take hold of and shape a generation for God. If they be timid time servers, place seekers; if they be men pleasers or men fearers; if their faith has a weak hold on God or His Word; if their denial be broken by any phase of self or the world, they cannot take hold of the Church nor the world for God.

The preacher's sharpest and strongest preaching should be to himself. His most difficult, delicate, laborious, thorough work must be with himself. The training of the twelve apostles was the great, difficult, and enduring work of Christ.

Preachers are not sermon makers, but men makers, and saint makers, and he only is well trained for this business who has made himself a man and a saint. It is neither great talents nor great learning nor great preachers that God needs but men great in holiness, great in faith, great in love, great in fidelity, great for God—men always preaching by holy sermons in the pulpit, by holy lives out of it. These can mold a generation for God.

Real Sermons Are Made in the Closet

The man—God's man—*is made in the closet*. His life and his profoundest convictions were born in his secret communion with God. The burdened and tearful agony of his spirit, his weightiest and sweetest messages were got when alone with God.

Prayer makes the man; prayer makes the preacher; prayer makes the pastor. The pulpit of this day is weak in praying. The pride of learning is against the dependent humility of prayer. Prayer is with the pulpit too often only official—a performance for the routine of service. Prayer is not to the modern pulpit the mighty force it was in Paul's life or Paul's ministry.

Every preacher who does not make prayer a mighty factor in his own life and ministry is weak as a factor in God's work and is powerless to project God's cause in this world.

The Spirit Alone Gives Life

The preaching that kills is *non spiritual* preaching. The ability of the preaching is not from God. Lower sources than God give to it energy and stimulant. The Spirit is not evident in the preacher nor in his preaching.

Many kinds of forces may be projected and stimulated by *preaching that kills*, but they're not spiritual forces. *The preaching that kills* is the letter; shapely and orderly it may be, but it is the letter still, the dry, husky letter, the empty, bald shell. The letter may have the germ of life in it, but it has no breath of spring to evoke it. Winter seeds they are, as hard as the winter's soil, as icy as the winter's air, no thawing nor germinating by them.

This letter preaching has the truth. But even divine truth has no life giving energy alone; it must be energized by the Spirit, with all God's forces at its back.

Truth unquickened by God's Spirit deadens as much as, or more than, error. It may be the truth without admixture; but without the Spirit its shade and touch are deadly, its truth error, its light darkness. The letter preaching is unctionless, neither mellowed nor oiled by the Spirit.

There may be tears, but tears cannot run God's machinery; tears may be but the summer's breath on a snow covered iceberg, nothing but surface slush. Feelings and earnestness there may be, but it is the emotion of the actor and the earnestness of the attorney.

The preacher may feel from the kindling of his own sparks. He may be eloquent over his own exegesis, and earnest in delivering the product of his own brain. The professor may usurp the place and imitate the fire of the apostle; brains and nerves may serve the place and feign the work of God's Spirit, and by these forces the letter may glow and sparkle like an illumined text—but the glow and sparkle will be as barren of life as the field sown with pearls. The death dealing element lies back of the words, back of the sermon, back of the occasion, back of the manner, back of the action. The great hindrance *is in the preacher himself.* He has not in himself the mighty life creating forces. There may be no discount on his orthodoxy, honesty, cleanness, or earnestness; but somehow the man, the inner man, in its secret places has never been broken down and surrendered to God. His inner life is not a great highway for the transmission of God's message, or God's power.

Somehow self, and not God, rules in the holy of holies. Somewhere, all unconscious to himself, some spiritual non conductor has touched his inner being, and the divine current has been arrested. His inner being has never felt its thorough spiritual bankruptcy, its utter powerlessness. He has never learned to cry out with an ineffable cry of self despair and self helplessness till God's power and God's fire comes in and fills, purifies, empowers. Self esteem, self ability in some pernicious shape has defamed and violated the temple, which should be held sacred for God.

God Uses Crucified Men

Life giving preaching costs the preacher much — death to self, crucifixion to the world, the travail of his own soul. Only crucified preaching can give life. Crucified preaching can come only from a crucified man.

The preaching that kills may be, and so often is, orthodox — dogmatically, inviolably orthodox. We love orthodoxy. It is good. It is the best. It is the clean, clear cut teaching of God's Word, the trophies won by truth in its conflict with error, and the levies which faith has raised against the desolating floods of honest or reckless misbelief or unbelief. But orthodoxy, clear, and hard as crystal, suspicious and militant, may be but *the letter* — well shaped, well named, and well learned — *the letter which kills.* Nothing is so dead as a dead orthodoxy, too dead to speculate, too dead to think, to study, or to pray.

The preaching that kills may have insight and grasp of principles. It may be scholarly and critical in taste, and may have every minutia of the derivation and grammar of the letter. It may be able to trim the letter to its perfect pattern, illuminate it as Plato and Cicero may be lumined, and may study it as a lawyer studies his textbooks to form his brief or to defend his case — and yet be like a frost, a killing frost.

Letter preaching may be eloquent, enameled with poetry and rhetoric, sprinkled with prayer, spiced with sensation, illumined by genius, and yet these be but the massive or chaste costly mountings, the rare and beautiful flowers which coffin the corpse.

The preaching that kills may be without scholarship, unmarked by any freshness of feeling or thought, clothed in tasteless generalities or vapid specialties, with style irregular, slovenly, saving neither of closet nor of study, graced neither by thought, expression, or prayer. Under such preaching how wide and utter the desolation—how profound the spiritual death!

Preaching That Kills is Prayerless Preaching

Without prayer the preacher creates death, and not life. The preacher who is *feeble in prayer* is *feeble in life giving forces*. The preacher who has retired prayer as a conspicuous and largely prevailing element in his own character has shorn his preaching of its distinctive life giving power.

Professional praying there is and will be, but professional praying helps the preaching to its deadly work. Professional praying chills and kills both preaching and praying. Much of the lax devotion and lazy, irreverent attitudes in congregational praying are attributable to professional praying in the pulpit. Long, discursive, dry, and inane are the prayers in many pulpits. Without unction or heart, they fall like a killing frost on all the graces of worship. Death dealing prayers they are. Every vestige of devotion has perished under their breath. The more dead they are the longer they grow.

A plea for short praying, life praying, real heart praying, praying by the Holy Spirit—direct, specific, ardent, simple, unctious in the pulpit—is in order. A school to teach ministers how to pray, as God counts praying, will be more beneficial to true piety, true worship, and true preaching than all theological schools.

The Preacher Must Be a Man of Prayer

Mr. Spurgeon says, "Of course the preacher is above all others distinguished as a man of prayer. He prays as an ordinary Christian, else he were a hypocrite. He prays more than ordinary Christians, else he were disqualified for the office he has undertaken.

If you as a minister are not very prayerful, you ought to be pitied. If you become lax in sacred devotion, not only will you need to be pitied but your people also, and the day cometh in which you shall be ashamed and confounded. All our libraries and studies are mere emptiness compared with our closets. Our seasons of fasting and prayer at the Tabernacle have been high days indeed; never has heaven's gate stood wider, never have our hearts been nearer the central glory."

Prayer is not a little habit pinned on to us while we were tied to our mother's apron strings; neither is it a little decent quarter of a minute's grace said over an hour's dinner, but it is a most serious work of our most serious years. It engages more of time and appetite than our longest dinings or richest feasts.

The prayer that makes much of our preaching must be made much of.

The character of our praying will determine the character of our preaching. Light praying will make light preaching. Prayer makes preaching strong, gives it unction, and makes it stick. In every ministry weighty for good, prayer has always been a serious business.

The preacher must be preeminently a man of prayer. His heart must graduate in the school of prayer. In the school of prayer only can the heart learn to preach. No learning can make up for the failure to pray. No earnestness, no diligence, no study, no gifts will supply its lack.

Talking to men for God is a great thing, but talking to God for men is greater still. He will never talk well and with real success to men for God who has not learned well how to talk to God for men. More than this, prayerless words in the pulpit and out of it are deadening words.

Prayer, in the preacher's life, in the preacher's study, in the preacher's pulpit, must be a conspicuous and an all impregnating force and an all coloring ingredient. It must play no secondary part, be no mere coating. To him it is given to be with his Lord "all night in prayer." The preacher to train himself in self denying prayer, is charged to look to his Master, who, "rising up a great while before day, went out, and departed into a solitary place, and there prayed." The preacher's study ought to be a closet, a Bethel, an altar, a vision, and a ladder, that every thought might ascend heavenward before it went manward; that every part of the sermon might be scented by the air of heaven and be made serious, because God was in the study.

As the engine never moves until the fire is kindled, so preaching, with all its machinery, perfection, and polish, is at a dead standstill as far as spiritual results are concerned, till prayer has kindled and created the steam. The texture, fineness, and strength of the sermon is as so much rubbish unless the mighty impulse of prayer is in it, through it, and behind it.

The Preacher Must, by Prayer, Put God in the Sermon

The preacher must, by prayer, move God toward the people, before he can move the people to God by his words. The preacher must have had audience and ready access to God before he can have access to the people. An open way to God for the preacher is the surest pledge of an open way to the people.

It is necessary to iterate and reiterate that prayer, as a mere habit, as a performance gone through by routine or in a professional way, is a dead and rotten thing. Such praying has no connection with the praying for which we plead.

Oneness with Christ Gives Birth to True Prayer

We are stressing true praying, which engages and sets on fire every high element of the preacher's being—prayer which is born of vital oneness with Christ and the fullness of the Holy Ghost. It springs from the deep, overflowing fountains of tender compassion and deathless solicitude for man's eternal good. It is a consuming zeal for the glory of God, a further conviction of the preacher's difficult and delicate work and of the imperative need of God's mightiest help.

Praying grounded on these solemn and profound convictions is the only *true praying*. Preaching backed by such praying is the only preaching which sows the seeds of eternal life in human hearts and builds men up for heaven. The preachers who gain mighty results for God are the men who have prevailed in their pleadings with God before venturing to plead with men.

The preachers who are the mightiest *in their closets with God* are the mightiest *in their pulpits with men.*

Preachers are human folks, and are exposed to and often caught by the strong driftings of human currents. Praying is spiritual work; and human nature does not like taxing, spiritual work. Human nature wants to sail to heaven under a favoring breeze, a full, smooth sea. Prayer is humbling work. It abases intellect and pride, crucifies vain glory, and signs our spiritual bankruptcy, and all these are hard for flesh and blood to bear. It is easier not to pray than to bear them.

So we come to one of the crying evils of these times, maybe of all times—*little or no praying.* Of these two evils, perhaps little praying is worse than no praying. Little praying is a kind of make believe, a salve for the conscience, a farce and a delusion.

The preacher is commissioned to pray as well as to preach. His mission is incomplete if he does not do both well. The preacher may speak with all eloquence of men and of angels; but unless he can pray with a faith that draws all heaven to his aid, his preaching will be "as sounding brass or a tinkling cymbal" for permanent, God honoring, soul saving uses.

Prayer which is felt as a mighty force is the mediate or immediate product of much time spent with God. Our short prayers owe their point and efficiency to the long ones that have preceded them. The short prevailing prayer cannot be prayed by one who has not prevailed with God in a mightier struggle of long continuance. Jacob's victory of faith could not have been gained without that all night wrestling. God's acquaintance is not made by pop calls. God does not bestow His gifts on the hasty comers and goers. Much time with God alone is the secret of knowing Him and of influencing with Him. He yields to the persistency of a faith that knows Him.

The men who have most fully illustrated Christ in their character, and have most powerfully affected the world for Him, have been men who have spent so much time with God as to make it a notable feature in their lives.

Charles Simeon — devoted the hours from four to eight in the morning to God.

John Wesley — spent two hours daily in prayer. He began at four in the morning. Of him, one who knew him well wrote: "He thought prayer to be his business more than anything else, and I have seen him come out of his closet with a serenity of face next to shining."

John Fletcher—stained the walls of his room by the breath of his prayers. Sometimes he would pray all night; always, frequently, and with great earnestness. His whole life was a life of prayer. "I would not rise from my seat," he said, "without lifting my heart to God." His greeting to a friend was always: "Do I meet you praying?"

Martin Luther—said, "If I fail to spend two hours in prayer each morning, the devil gets the victory through the day. I have so much business I cannot get on without spending three hours daily in prayer." He had a motto: "He that has prayed well has studied well."

Archbishop Leighton—was so much alone with God that he seemed to be in perpetual meditation. "Prayer and praise were his business and his pleasure," says his biographer.

Bishop Ken—was so much with God that his soul was said to be God enamored. He was with God before the clock struck three every morning.

Bishop Asbury—said, "I propose to rise at four o'clock as often as I can and spend two hours in prayer and meditation."

Samuel Rutherford—the fragrance of whose piety is still rich, rose at three in the morning to meet God in prayer.

Joseph Alleine—arose at four o'clock for this business of praying till eight. If he heard other tradesmen plying their business before he was up, he would exclaim, "Oh, how this shames me! Doth not my Master deserve more than theirs?"

He who has learned this trade well draws at will, on sight, and with acceptance of heaven's unfailing bank.

John Welch—the holy and wonderful Scottish preacher, thought the day ill spent if he did not spend eight or ten hours in prayer.

Bishop Wilson—says, "In Henry Martyn's journal, the spirit of prayer, the time he devoted to the duty, and his fervor in it are the finest things which strike me."

Edward Payson—wore the hard wood boards into grooves where his knees pressed so often and so long. His biographer says, "His continuing instant in prayer, be his circumstances what they might, is the most noticeable fact in his history, and points out the duty of all who would rival his eminency. To his ardent and persevering prayers must no doubt be ascribed in a great measure his distinguished and almost uninterrupted success."

The Marquis DeRenty — to whom Christ was most precious, ordered his servant to call him from his devotions at the end of half an hour. The servant at the time saw his face through an aperture. It was marked with such holiness that he hated to arouse him. His lips were moving, but he was perfectly silent. He waited until three half hours had passed; then he called to him. When he arose from his knees, he said that the half hour was so short when he was communing with Christ.

David Brainerd — said, "I love to be alone in my cottage, where I can spend much time in prayer."

William Bramwell — is famous in Methodist annals for personal holiness and for his wonderful success in preaching and for the marvelous answers to his prayers. For hours at a time he would pray. He almost lived on his knees. He went over his circuits like a flame of fire. The fire was kindled by the time he spent in prayer. He often spent as much as four hours in a single season of prayer in retirement.

Bishop Andrewes — spent the greatest part of five hours every day in prayer and devotion.

Sir Henry Havelock—always spent the first two hours of the day alone with God. If the encampment was struck at six a.m., he would rise at four.

Earl Cairns—rose daily at six o'clock to secure an hour and a half for the study of the Bible and for prayer before conducting family worship at a quarter to eight.

Adoniram Judson's—success in prayer is attributable to the fact that he gave much time to prayer. He says on this point: "Arrange thy affairs, if possible, so that thou canst leisurely devote two or three hours every day not merely to devotional exercises but to the very act of secret prayer and communion with God. Endeavor seven times a day to withdraw from business and company and lift thy soul to God in private retirement.

"Begin the day by rising after midnight and devoting some time amid the silence of darkness of the night to this sacred work. Let the hour of opening dawn find thee at the same work. Let the hours of nine, twelve, three, six, and nine at night witness the same. Be resolute in His cause. Make all practicable sacrifices to maintain it. Consider that thy time is short, and that business and company must not be allowed to rob thee of thy God."

Impossible, we say, *fanaticable directions!* Dr. Judson impressed an empire for Christ and laid the foundation of God's kingdom with imperishable granite in the heart of Burma.

Judson was successful—one of the few men who mightily impressed the world for Christ. Many men have greater gifts and genius and learning and have made no such impression; their religious work is like footsteps in the sands, but he has engraven his work on the adamant.

Everywhere, everything in apostolic times was on the stretch that the people of God might each and "all come in the unity of the faith, and of the knowledge of the Son of God, unto a perfect man, unto the measure of the stature of the fullness of Christ." No premium was given to dwarfs; no encouragement to an old babyhood. The babies were to grow; the old, instead of feebleness and infirmities, were to bear fruit in old age, and be fat and flourishing.

The most divine thing in religion is holy men and holy women. No amount of money, genius, or culture can move things for God.

Holiness energizing the souls, the whole man aflame with love, with desire for more faith, more prayer, more zeal, more consecration—this is the secret of power. These we need and must have, and men must be the incarnation of this God inflamed devotedness. God's advance has been stayed, His cause crippled, His name dishonored for their lack.

Genius (though the loftiest and most gifted), education (though the most learned and refined), position, dignity, place, honored names, high ecclesiastics cannot move this chariot of our God. It is a fiery one, and only fiery forces can move it.

The genius of a Milton fails. The imperial strength of a Leo fails. However, Brainerd's spirit can move it! Brainerd's spirit was on fire for God, on fire for souls. Nothing earthly, worldly, selfish came in to abate in the least the intensity of this all impelling and all consuming force and flame.

The Unity of Devotion and Prayer

Prayer is the creator as well as the channel of devotion. The spirit of devotion is the spirit of prayer. Prayer and devotion are united as soul and body are united, as life and heart are united. There is no real prayer without devotion, no devotion without prayer.

The preacher must be surrendered to God in the holiest devotion. He is not a professional man, his ministry is not a profession; it is a divine institution, a divine devotion. The preacher, above everything else, must be devoted to God.

The preacher's relations to God are the insignia and credentials of his ministry. They must be clear, conclusive and unmistakable. No common, surface type of piety must be his. If he does not excel in grace, he does not excel at all. If he does not preach by life, character, conduct, he does not preach at all. If his piety be light, his preaching may be as soft and as sweet as music, as gifted as Apollo, yet its weight will be a feather's weight, visionary, fleeting as the morning cloud or the early dew.

Never did the cause of God need perfect illustrations of the possibilities of prayer more than in this age. No age, no person, will be examples of the gospel power except the ages or persons of deep and earnest prayer. A prayerless age will have but scant models of divine power. Prayerless hearts will never rise to these Alpine heights.

The age may be a better age than the past, but there is an infinite distance between the betterment of an age by the force of advancing civilization and its betterment by the increase of holiness and Christ-likeness by the energy of prayer. The Jews were much better when Christ came than in the ages before. It was the golden age of their Pharisaic religion. Their golden religious age crucified Christ. Never more praying, never less praying; never more sacrifices, never less sacrifice; never more idolatry, never less idolatry; never more of temple worship, never less of God worship; never more of lip service, never less of heart service (God worship by lips whose hearts and hands crucified God's Son); never more of churchgoers, never less of saints.

A prayer force makes saints. Holy characters are formed by the power of real praying. The more of true saints, the more of true praying; the more of true praying, the more of true saints. The men of mighty prayer are men of spiritual might.

Prayers Never Die

Brainerd's whole life was a life of prayer. By day and by night he prayed. Before preaching and after preaching he prayed. Riding through the interminable solitude of the forests he prayed. On his bed of straw he prayed. Retiring to the dense and lonely forests he prayed. Hour by hour, day after day, early morn and late at night, he was praying and fasting, pouring out his soul, interceding, communing with God. He was with God mightily in prayer, and God was with him mightily, and by it he being dead yet speaketh and worketh, and will speak and work till the end comes, and among the glorious ones of that glorious day he will be with the first.

Jonathan Edwards says of him; "His life shows the right way to success in the works of the ministry. He sought it as a soldier seeks victory in a siege or battle; or as a man who runs a race for a great prize. Animated with love to Christ and souls, how did he labor? Always fervently. Not only in words and doctrine, in public and in private, but in prayers by day and night, wrestling with God in secret and travailing in birth with unutterable groans and agonies, until Christ was formed in the hearts of the people to whom he was sent. Like a true son of Jacob, he persevered in wrestling all through the dark hours of the night, until the breaking of the day."

The Preacher Must Be Prayed For

Prayer, with its manifold and many sided forces, helps the mouth to utter the truth in its fullness and freedom. The preacher is to be prayed for. The preacher is made by prayer. The preacher's mouth is to be prayed for; his mouth is to be opened and filled by prayer. A holy mouth is made by praying, by much praying; a brave mouth is made by praying, by much praying. The Church and the world, God and heaven, owe much to Paul's mouth; Paul's mouth owed its power to prayer. How manifold, illimitable, valuable, and helpful prayer is to the preacher in so many ways, at so many points, in every way!

The Prepared Heart

One great value [of prayer] is, it helps his heart. Praying makes the preacher a heart preacher. Prayer puts the preacher's heart into the preacher's sermon; prayer puts the preacher's sermon into the preacher's heart. The heart makes the preacher. Men of great hearts are great preachers. Men of bad hearts may do a measure of good, but this is rare.

We have emphasized sermon preparation until we have lost sight of the important thing to be prepared—*the heart.*

A prepared heart is much better than a prepared sermon. A prepared heart will make a prepared sermon.

Volumes have been written, laying down the mechanics and taste of sermon making, until we have become possessed with the idea that this scaffolding is the building. The young preacher has been taught to layout all his strength on the form, taste and beauty of his sermon as a mechanical and intellectual product. We have thereby cultivated a vicious taste among the people and raise the clamor for talent instead of grace, eloquence instead of piety, rhetoric instead of revelation, reputation and brilliancy instead of holiness. By it we have lost the true idea of preaching, lost preaching power, lost pungent conviction for sin, lost the rich experience and elevated Christian character, lost the authority over consciences and lives which always result from genuine preaching.

It would not do to say that preachers study too much. Some of them do not study at all; others do not study enough. Numbers do not study the right way to show themselves workmen approved of God. But our great lack is not in head culture, but in heart culture; not lack of knowledge, but lack of holiness is our sad and telling defect—not that we know too much, but that we do not meditate on God and His Word and watch and fast and pray enough.

The heart is the great hindrance to our preaching. Words pregnant with divine truth find in our hearts nonconductors; arrested, they fall shorn and powerless.

Can ambition that lusts after praise and place preach the gospel of Him who made himself of no reputation and took on Him the form of a servant? Can the proud, the vain, the egotistical, preach the gospel of Him who was meek and lowly; can the bad tempered, passionate, selfish, hard, worldly man preach the system which teems with long suffering, self denial, tenderness, which imperatively demands separation from enmity and crucifixion to the world?

The Heart is the Savior of the World

Heads do not save. Genius, brains, brilliancy, strength, natural gifts do not save. The gospel flows through hearts. All the mightiest forces are heart forces. All the sweetest and loveliest graces are heart graces. Great hearts make great characters; great hearts make divine characters.

God is love. There is nothing greater than love, nothing greater than God. Hearts make heaven; heaven is love. There is nothing higher, nothing sweeter, than heaven. It is the heart, and not the head, which makes God's great preachers. The heart counts much every way in religion. The heart must speak from the pulpit. The heart must hear in the pew. In fact, we serve God with our hearts. Head homage does not pass current in heaven.

Unction is the Art of Preaching

The preacher who never had this unction never had the art of preaching. The preacher who has lost this unction has lost the art of preaching. Whatever other arts he may have and retain—the art of sermon making, the art of eloquence, the art of great, clear thinking, the art of pleasing an audience—he has lost the divine art of preaching. This unction makes God's truth powerful and interesting, draws and attracts, edifies, convicts, saves. This unction vitalizes God's revealed truth, makes it living and life giving.

Even God's truth spoken without this anointing is light, dead and deadening. Though abounding in truth, though weighty with thought, though sparkling with rhetoric, though pointed by logic and though powerful by earnestness, without this divine unction it issues in death and not life.

Mr. Spurgeon says: "I wonder how long we might beat our brains before we could plainly put into words what is meant by preaching with unction. Yet he who preaches knows its presence and he who hears soon detects its absence.

Samaria in famine typifies a discourse without it. Jerusalem, with her feast of fat things, full of marrow, may represent a sermon enriched with it. Everyone knows what the freshness of the morning is when Orient pearls abound on every blade of grass, but who can describe it, much less produce it of itself? Such is the mystery of spiritual anointing. We know, but we cannot tell to others what it is. It is as easy as it is foolish, to counterfeit it. Unction is a thing which you cannot manufacture, and its counterfeits are worse than worthless. Yet it is, in itself, priceless, and beyond measure needful if you would edify believers and bring sinners to Christ. "

Unction is that indefinable, indescribable something which an old, renowned Scotch preacher described thus: "There is sometimes somewhat in preaching that cannot be described either to matter or to expression, and cannot be described what it is, or from whence it cometh, but with a sweet violence it pierces into the heart and affections and comes immediately from the Lord; but if there be any way to obtain such a thing, it is by the heavenly disposition of the speaker." We call it *unction.*

It is this unction which makes the Word of God *"quick, and powerful, and sharper than any two edged sword, piercing even to the dividing asunder of soul and spirit, and of the joints and marrow, and is a discerner of the thoughts and intents of the heart."*

It is this unction which gives the words of the preacher such point, sharpness, and power, and which creates such friction and stir in many a dead congregation.

The same truths have been told in the strictness of the letter, smooth as human oil could make them; but no signs of life, not a pulse throb; all as peaceful as the grave and as dead.

The same preacher in the meanwhile receives the baptism of this unction, the divine inflatus is upon him, the letter of the Word has been embellished and fired by this mysterious power, and the throbbings of life begin—life which receives or life which resists. The unction pervades and convicts the conscience and breaks the heart.

Unction is simply putting God in His own Word and on His own preacher. By mighty, great, continual prayerfulness, it is all potential and personal to the preacher. It inspires and clarifies his intellect. It gives insight and grasp and protecting power. It gives the preacher heart power—which is greater than head power. Tenderness, purity, and force flow from the heart by it. Enlargement, freedom, fullness of thought, directness and simplicity of utterance are the fruits of this unction.

Earnestness is not Unction

Earnestness and unction look alike from some points of view. Earnestness may be readily and without detection substituted or mistaken for unction. It requires a spiritual eye and a spiritual taste to discriminate.

Earnestness may be sincere, serious, ardent, and persevering. It goes at a thing with good will, pursues it with perseverance, and urges it with ardor; puts force in it. But all these forces do not rise higher than the mere human:

The man is in it—*the whole man*, with all that he has of will and heart, of brain and genius, of planning, working, and talking.

He has set himself to some purpose, which has mastered him, and he pursues to master it. There may be none of God in it. There may be little of God in it, because there is so much of the man in it.

It was said of a rather famous preacher of gifts, whose construction of Scripture was to his fancy or purpose, that he "grew very eloquent over his own exegesis." So men grow exceeding earnest over their own plans or movements. Earnestness may be selfishness simulated.

What of unction? It is the indefinable in preaching which makes it *preaching*. It is that which distinguishes and separates preaching from all mere human addresses. It is the divine in preaching. It makes the preaching sharp to those who need sharpness. It distills as the dew to those who need to be refreshed. It is well described as:

> " ... *a two edged sword*
> *Of heavenly temper keen,*
> *And double were the wounds it made*
> *Where're it glanced between.*
> *'Twas death to sin; 'Twas life*
> *To all who mourned for sin.*
> *It kindled and it silenced strife,*
> *Made war and peace within.*"

This unction comes to the preacher not in the study but in the closet. It is heaven's distillation in answer to prayer.

It is the sweetest exhalation of the Holy Spirit. It impregnates, suffuses, softens, percolates, cuts, and soothes. It carries the Word like dynamite, like salt, like sugar; makes the Word a soother, and arraigner, a revealer, a searcher; makes the hearer a culprit or a saint, makes him weep like a child and live like a giant; opens his heart and his purse as gently, yet as strongly, as the spring opens the leaves.

This unction is not the gift of genius. It is not found in the halls of learning. No eloquence can woo it. No industry can win it. No prelatical hands can confer it. It is the gift of God—the signet set to His own messengers. It is heaven's knighthood given to the chosen, true, and brave ones who have sought this anointed honor through many an hour of tearful, wrestling prayer. Earnestness is good and impressive; genius is gifted and great; thought kindles and inspires. But it takes a more divine endowment, a more powerful energy than earnestness or genius or thought to break the chains of sin, to win the estranged and depraved hearts to God, to repair the breaches and restore the Church to her old ways of purity and power.

Nothing but this holy unction can do this.

Unction is the Anointing of the Holy Ghost

In the Christian system unction is the anointing of the Holy Ghost, separating unto God's work and qualifying for it. This unction is the one divine enablement by which the preacher accomplishes the peculiar and saving ends of preaching. Without this unction there are no true spiritual results accomplished; the results and forces in preaching do not rise above the results of unsanctified speech. Without unction the former is as potent as the pulpit.

This divine unction on the preacher generates through the Word of God the spiritual results that flow from the gospel; and without this unction, these results are not secured. Many pleasant impressions may be made, but these all fall far below the ends of gospel preaching.

This unction may be simulated. There are many things that look like it, there are many results that resemble its effects; but they are foreign to its results and to its nature. The fervor or softness excited by a pathetic or emotional sermon may look like the movements of the divine unction, but they have no pungent, penetrating, heart breaking force. No heart healing balm is there in these surface, sympathetic, emotional movements; they are not radical, neither sin searching nor sin curing.

This divine unction is the one distinguishing feature that separates true gospel preaching from all other methods of presenting truth. It backs and interpenetrates the revealed truth with all the force of God. It illumines the Word and broadens and enriches the intellect and empowers it to grasp and apprehend the Word. It qualifies the preacher's heart, and brings it to that condition of tenderness, of purity, of force and light that are necessary to secure the highest results. This unction gives to the preacher liberty and enlargement of thought and soul—a freedom, a fullness, and directness of utterance that can be secured by no other process.

This unction, the divine unction, this heavenly anointing, is what the pulpit needs and must have. This divine and heavenly oil put on by the imposition of God's hand must soften and lubricate the whole man—heart, head, spirit—until it separates him from selfish motives and aims, separating him to everything that is pure and God-like.

The Heavenly Oil of Unction is a Conditional Gift

This unction is not an inalienable gift. It is a conditional gift. Its presence is perpetuated and increased by the same process by which it was first secured; by unceasing prayer to God, by impassioned desires after God, by estimating it, by seeking it with tireless ardor, and by deeming all else loss and failure without it.

How and whence comes this unction? Direct from God in answer to prayer. Praying hearts only are the hearts filled with this holy oil; praying lips only are anointed with this divine unction.

Prayer, much prayer, is the price of preaching unction; prayer, much prayer, is the one sole condition of keeping this unction. Without unceasing prayer, the unction never comes to the preacher. Without perseverance in prayer, the unction, like the manna over kept, breeds worms.

The apostles knew the necessity and worth of prayer to their ministry. They knew that their high commission as apostles, instead of relieving them from the necessity of prayer, committed them to it by a more urgent need, so that they were exceedingly jealous else some other important work should exhaust their time and prevent their praying as they ought; so they appointed laymen to look after the delicate and engrossing duties of ministering to the poor, that they (the apostles) might, unhindered, "give themselves continually to prayer and to the ministry of the word."

Prayer is put first, and their relation to prayer is put most strongly—"give themselves to it," making a business of it, surrendering themselves to praying, putting fervor, urgency, perseverance, and time in it. How holy, apostolic men devoted themselves to this divine work of prayer! "Night and day praying exceedingly," says Paul. "We will give ourselves continually to prayer" is the consensus of apostolic devotement. How these New Testament preachers laid themselves out in prayer for God's people! How they put God in force into their churches by their praying!

These holy apostles did not vainly fancy that they had met their high and solemn duties by delivering faithfully God's Word, but their preaching was made to stick and tell by the ardor and insistence of their praying.

Apostolic praying was as taxing, toilsome and imperative as apostolic preaching. They prayed mightily day and night to bring their people to the highest regions of faith and holiness. Apostolic praying makes apostolic saints and keeps apostolic times of purity and power in the Church.

Preachers Are Preeminently God's Leaders

Preachers are primarily responsible for the condition of the Church. They shape its character and give tone and direction to its life. Much every way depends on these leaders. They shape the times and the institutions. The Church is divine, the treasure it incases is heavenly, but it bears the imprint of the human.

The treasure is in earthen vessels, and it smacks of the vessel. The Church of God makes, or is made by, its leaders. Whether it makes them or is made by them, it will be what its leaders are; spiritual if they are so, secular if they are, conglomerate if its leaders are.

Israel's kings gave character to Israel's piety. A church rarely revolts against or rises above the religion of its leaders. A prayerless ministry is the undertaker for all God's truth and for God's Church.

Prayer, to the preacher, is not simply the duty of his profession, a privilege, but it is a necessity. Air is not more necessary to the lungs than prayer is to the preacher. It is absolutely necessary for the preacher to pray. It is an absolute necessity that the preacher be prayed for.

These two propositions are wedded into a union which ought never to know any divorce: the preacher must pray; the preacher must be prayed for. It will take all the praying he can do, and all the praying he can get done, to meet the fearful responsibilities and gain the largest, truest success in his great work.

The more the preacher's eyes are opened to the nature, responsibility, and difficulties in his work, the more will he see, and if he be a true preacher, the more will he feel, the necessity of prayer; not only the increasing demand to pray himself, but to call on others to help him by their prayers.

Paul is an illustration of this. If any man could project the gospel by dint of personal force, by brain power, by culture, by personal grace, by God's apostolic commission, God's extraordinary call, that man was Paul. That the preacher must be a man given to prayer, Paul is an eminent example.

That the true apostolic preacher must have the prayers of other good people to give to his ministry its full quota of success, Paul is a preeminent example. He asks, he covets, he pleads in an impassioned way for the help of all God's saints. He knew that in the spiritual realm, as elsewhere, in union there is strength; that the concentration and aggregation of faith, desire and prayer increased the volume of spiritual force until it became overwhelming and irresistible in its power.

Units of prayer combined, like drops of water, make an ocean that defies resistance. So Paul, with his clear and full apprehension of spiritual dynamics, determined to make his ministry as impressive, as eternal, as irresistible, as the ocean, that by gathering all the scattered units of prayer and precipitating them on his ministry. Called, commissioned, chief of the apostles as he was, all his equipment was imperfect without the prayers of his people. He wrote letters everywhere, urging them to pray for him.

Do You Pray For Your Preacher?

Do you pray for him in secret? Public prayers are of little worth unless they are founded on or followed up by private praying. Our devotions are not measured by the clock but time is of their essence. The ability to wait and stay and press belongs essentially to our intercourse with God.

Hurry, everywhere unseeming and damaging, is so to an alarming extent in the great business of a communion with God. Short devotions are the bane of deep piety. Calmness, grasp, strength, are never the companions of hurry. Short devotions deplete spiritual vigor, arrest spiritual progress, sap spiritual foundations and blight the root and bloom of spiritual life. They are the prolific source of backsliding, the sure indication of a superficial piety; they deceive, blight, rot the seed, and impoverish the soil.

It is true that Bible prayers in word and print are short, but the praying men of the Bible were with God through many a sweet and holy wrestling hour. They won by few words but long waiting. The prayers Moses records may be short, but Moses prayed to God with fastings and mighty cryings forty days and nights.

The statement of Elijah's praying may be condensed to a few brief paragraphs, but doubtless Elijah, who, when "praying he prayed," spent many hours of fiery struggle and lofty intercourse with God before he could, with assured boldness, say to Ahab, "There shall not be dew nor rain these years, but according to my word."

The verbal brief of Paul's prayers is short, but Paul "prayed night and day exceedingly."

The Lord's Prayer is a divine epitome for infant lips, but the Man Christ Jesus prayed many an all night before His work was done; and His all night and long sustained devotions gave to His work its finish and perfection, and to His character the fullness and glory of its divinity.

Spiritual work is taxing work, and men are loath to do it. Praying, true praying, costs an outlay of serious attention and of time, which flesh and blood do not relish. Few persons are made of such strong fiber that they will make a costly outlay when surface work will pass as well in the market.

To Be Little with God is to Be Little For God

To cut short the praying makes the whole religious character short, scrimp and slovenly. William Wilberforce, the peer of kings, said: "I must secure more time for private devotions. I have been living far too public for me. The shortening of private devotions starves the soul; it grows lean and faint. I have been keeping too late hours."

We must learn anew the worth of prayer, enter anew the school of prayer.

There is nothing which it takes more time to learn. And if we would learn the wondrous art, we must not give a fragment here and there, "a little talk with Jesus," as the tiny *saintlets* sing—but we must demand and hold with iron grasp the best hours of the day for God and prayer, or there will be no praying worth the name.

Who prays as Jacob prayed—till he is crowned as a prevailing, princely intercessor? Who prays as Elijah prayed—till all the locked up forces of nature were unsealed and the famine stricken land bloomed as the garden of God?

Who prayed as Jesus Christ prayed—as out upon the mountain He "continued all night in prayer to God"? The apostles "gave themselves to prayer"—the most difficult thing to get a man or even the preachers to do. Laymen there are who will give their money— some of them in rich abundance—but they will not "give themselves" to prayer, without which their money is but a curse.

There are plenty of preachers who will deliver great and eloquent addresses on the need of revival and the spread of the kingdom of God, but not many there are who will do that without which all preaching and organizing are worse than vain—*pray*. It is out of date, almost a lost art, and the greatest benefactor this age could have is a man who will bring the preachers and the Church back to prayer.

My creed leads me to think that prayer is efficacious, and surely a day's asking God to overrule all events is not lost. Still there is a great feeling that when a man is praying he is *doing nothing,* and this feeling makes us give undue importance to work— sometimes even to the hurrying over or even to the neglect of prayer.

Do not we rest in our day too much on the arm of flesh? Cannot the same wonders be done now as of old? Do not the eyes of the Lord run to and fro throughout the whole earth still to shew himself strong on behalf of those who put their trust in Him? Oh! That God would give me more practical faith in Him. Where is now the Lord God of Elijah? HE IS WAITING FOR ELIJAH TO CALL ON HIM!

Notes

Good Preaching, by Glenn Conjurske:

1. Memoirs of Charles G. Finney, written by himself; New York: A,S, Barnes & Company, n.d., pg. 369.

2. Sermons on Gospel Themes, by Charles Finney; New York: Fleming H. Revell Company, n.d., pg 268.

3. (2) ibid., pg 270.

4. The Letters of John Wesley, edited by John Telford; London: The Epworth Press, 1931, Vol. V, pg. 345.

5. Sermons on Gospel Themes, pg. 187.

6. The Great Redemption; or, Gospel Light under the labor of Moody and Sankey (Sermons preached at the Cleveland Tabernacle in 1879); Chicago: The Century Book and Paper Co., 1889. pp. 85-86.

7. The Gospel Awakening" (Sermons by Moody),edited by L.T. Remlap; Chicago: J. Fairbanks Co.pg.317.

8. The Journal of Charles Wesley; Grand Rapids: Baker Book House, 1980, Vol. I, pg. 281

9. Charles Grandison Finney, by G. Frederick Wright; Boston and New York: Houghton, Mifflin and Company, 1891, pg. 282.

10. Sermon on Gospel Themes, pg. 213.

11. The Letters of John Wesley, Vol. III, pg. 34.

12. ibid., pp 79-80.

13. The Revival We Need, by Oswald J. Smith; London and Edinburgh: Marshall, Morgan & Scott, Ltd., n.d., pp.19-20.

14. The Life and Labors of Charles H. Spurgeon, by George C. Needham; Boston: D.L. Guernsey,1884; pg. 39.

15. Lectures to Professing Christians, by Charles G. Finney; London: Milner and Company, Limited, n.d., Pp. 95-96.

16. The Soul - Winner, by C. H. Spurgeon; London: Passmore & Alabaster, 1897, pg. 75.

17. Bud Robinson, by J. B. Chapman; Kansas City, Mo.: Beacon Hill Press, pp. 171-172.

18. ibid., pg. 172.

19. Memoirs of the Life of David Marks, edited by Mrs. Marilla Marks; Dover, N. H.: Free-Will Baptist Printing Establishment, 1846, pp. 39-40.

20. ibid., pg. 241.

21. The Life of Luther, written by himself; collected and arranged by M. Michelet; translated by William Hazlitt; London: David Bogue, 1846, pg. 126.

22. Life and Times of Girolamo Savonarola, by Pasquale Villari, translated by Linda Villari; London: T. Fisher Unwin, 1899, pg.79.

23. Personal Reminiscences of Charles Haddon Spurgeon, by W. Williams; London: The Religious Tract Society, 1895, pg.203.

24. Evangelistic Work in Principle and Practice, by Arthur T. Pierson; New York: The Baker and Taylor Co., n.d., pg.252.

25. Memoirs of Charles G. Finney, pg.88.

26. The Life of John Owen, by James Moffat; London: Congregational Union of England and Wales, n.d., pg.65.

27. The Life of George Whitefield, by L. Tyerman; London: Hodder and Stoughton, 1890, Vol. pg. 510.

28. 28 ibid., pg. 511.

29. Memories of George Whitefield, by John Gillies (Revised and Corrected with Large Additions and Improvements); Middletown: Hunt and Noyes, 1838, pg. 143.

30. The life of John Wesley, by John Whitehead; Boston: J. McLeish, 1844, Vol. I, pg. 228.

31. The life of John Wesley, by Henry Moore; New-York: Published by N. Bangs and J. Emory, for the Methodist Episcopal Church, 1825, Vol. II. Pp. 311-312.

32. The Journal of Charles Wesley, Vol. II, pg. 61.

33. Recollections of a Long Life, by T. L. Cuyler; New York: The American Tract Society, 1902, pg. 216.

34. Life of Charles G. Finney, by A. M. Hills; Cincinnati: Office of "God's Revivalist,"1902, pg. 39.

35. Memories of Charles G. Finney, pp. 100,101.

36. An Earnest Ministry the Want of the Rimes, by John Angell James; New York: M.W. Dodd, 1849,pg.170.

37. The Soul-Winner, pp. 74-75.

38. ibid., pg.183.

39. Memories of William Ripley; Philadelphia: J.H. Cunningham, 1827, pg. 70.

40. The Works of President Edwards: With a Memoir of His Life (by Sereno Edwards Dwight): New-York: S. Converse, 1829, Vol. 1, pp. 605-606.

41. ibid., pg. 607.

42. ibid., pp. 606-607.

43. An Earnest Ministry the Want of the Times, by John Angell James, pg. 112.

44. A narrative of Many Surprising Conversations in Northampton and Vicinity, by Jonathan Edwards; Worcester: Moses W. Grout, 1832, pg.12.

45. The Works of President Edwards, vol. I pg. 605.

46. Historical Collections Relating to remarkable Periods of the Success of the Gospel, and Eminent Instruments Employed in Promoting It, compiled by John Gillies; Glasgow: Robert and Andrew Foulis, 1754, Vol. II, pg. 169.

47. Witnessing to Jews, by Milton B. Lindberg; Chicago: Chicago Hebrew Mission, 1951, pg. 10.

48. The Journal of John Wesley; London & Toronto: J. M. Dent & Sons, 1922.

49. S. H. Hadley of Water Street, by J. Wilbur Chapman; New York: Fleming H. Revell Company, n.d., pg. 167.

50. ibid., pp. 98-99.

51. ibid., pg. 132.

52. ibid., pp. 134-135.

53. Appendix to George Whitefield's Journals; The Banner of Truth Trust, 1960, pp. 561-562.

54. C. H. Spurgeon's Autobiography, compiled by his wife and his private secretary; London: Passmore & Alabaster, Vol. II, 1898, pg. 99.

55. The Metropolitan Tabernacle: Its History and Work, by C. H. Spurgeon; London: Passmore & Alabaster, 1876, pg. 73.

56. Why God Used D. L. Moody, by R. A. Torrey; Chicago" The Bible Institute Colportage Ass'n, n. d., pp. 24-25.

57. Torrey and Alexander, by George T.B. Davis; London: James Nisbet & Co., Limited, n.d., pg. 101.

58. ibid., pp. 101-102.

59. The Real Billy Sunday, by Elijah P. Brown; New York: Fleming Revel Company, n.d., pp. 60-61.

60. A Select Collection of Letters of George Whitefield; London: Edward and Charles Dilly, 1772, Vol. 1, pg. 381.

61. ibid., Vol. II pg. 45.

62. ibid., pg. 71.

63. Life of Whitefield, by Tyerman, Vol. II, Pg. 393.

64. Sermons of Christmas Evans. With a Memoir and Portraiture of the Author, by Joseph Cross; Philadelphia; J. Harmstead, 1846, pg. 23.

65. Vol. I, pg.166.

66. ibid., pg. 294.

67. ibid. Vol. II. Pg. 104.

68. Savonarola, by Villari, pp. 309-310.

69. Memoirs of Marks, by his wife, pp. 500-501.

70. The life of John W. de la Flechere, by Joseph Benson; New York: Carlton & Phillips, 1855, pg. 136.

71. ibid., pg. 265.

72. The Journal of Francis Asbury; New-York: Published by N. Bangs and T. Mason, for the Methodist Episcopal Church, 1821, Vol. I, pg. 173.

73. The Great Awakening. A History of the Revival of Religion in the Time of Edwards and Whitefield, by Joseph Tracy; Boston: Tappan and Dennet, 1842, pg. 60.

74. Memoir of the Life and Character of Asahel Nettleton, by Bennet Tyler; Hartford: Robins and Smith, 1845, pg. 76.

75. Bringing In Sheaves, by A. B. Earle; Boston: James H. Earle, 1875, pg. 101.

76. Journal of Francis Asbury, Vol. I, pg. 162.

77. Memoir of Robert Haldane, and James Alexander Haldane, (anonymous); New York: American Tract Society, n.d., pp. 269-270.

78. The Lives of Early Methodist Preachers, edited by Thomas Jackson; London: Wesleyan Conference Office, 1875, Vol. I, pg. 61.

79. The Life of Freeborn Garretson, by Nathan Bangs; New York: Published by J. Emory an dB. Waugh, at the Conference Office, 1829, pg. 37.

80. Lectures on Revivals of Religion, by Charles G. Finney; Oberlin, Ohio: Published by E. J. Goodrich, n.d., pg. 342.

81. ibid., pg. 164.

82. Sermons on Gospel Themes, pg. 225.

83. The Life of Freeborn Garrettson, by Bangs, pg. 74.

84. Experience and Gospel Labors of Benjamin Abbott, compiled by John Ffirth; New-York: Carlton & Phillips, 1856, pg. 46.

85. Memoir of the Life and Ministry of William Bramwell, by James Sigston; New York: Phillips & Hunt, n.d., pg. 148.

86. An Earnest Ministry the Want of the Times, pg. 267.

87. Lectures on Revival of Religion, pg. 111.

88. ibid., pg.443.

89. Autobiography of Peter Cartwright, edited by W. P. Strickland; Cincinnati: Cranston and Curts, n.d. pp. 78-79.

90. ibid. pg. 408.

91. Sketches of Western Methodism, by James B. Finley, edited by W. P. Strickland; Cincinnati: printed at the Methodist Book Concern, for the Author, 1857, pg. 322. John Collins is the preacher described.

92. History of the Cumberland Presbyterian Church, by B. W. McDonnold; Nashville, Tenn.: Board of Publication of Cumberland Presbyterian Church, 1888, pg. 90

93. ibid, pg. 96.

94. Anecdotes and Illustrations, by R. A. Torrey; New York: Fleming H. Revell Company, n.d., pp.155-156.

95. The Model Preacher, by William Taylor; Cincinnati: Published by Poe & Hitchcock, for the Author, 1863, pg. 273.

96. Real Religion, by Gipsy Smith; London: Hodder and Stroughton. n.d., pg. 25.

97. Things New and Old, (edited by C. H. Mackintosh); London: G. Morrish. Vol. III, 1860, pp. 169-179.

98. Original Letters From John Newton to W. Barlass; New York: James Eastburn, and Co. 1819, pp. 149-150.

99. ibid,. pg. 165.

100. Letters of George Whitefield, Vol. II pg. 359.

101. Sermons on Important Subjects, by George Whitefield; London: William Tegg, 1867, Pg. 305.

102. The Early Life of Howeli Harris, by Richard Bennett, translated from the Welsh by Gomer M. Roberts; London: The Banner of Truth Trust, 1962, pg. 42.

103. Sixty Years an Evangelist: An intimate Study of Gipsy Smith, by Harold Murray; London & Edinburgh: Marshal, Morgan &Scott, Ltd., 1937, pg. 122.

104. Memoirs of Charles G. Finney, by himself, pg. 95.

105. Sixty Years an Evangelist, by Harold Murray, pg. 56.

106. ibid,. pg. 54.

107. Life of Fletcher, by Benson, pg. 138.

108. An All-Round Ministry, by C. H. Spurgeon; London: Passmore and Alabaster, 1900, pg. 356.

109. ibid., pp.183-184.

110. The Revivals of the Eighteenth Century, Particularly at Cambuslang.

111. Life of Whitefield, by Tyerman, Vol. II, pg. 393.

112. Memoirs of Whitefield, by Gillies, pg.285.

113. Fifty years as a Presiding Elder, by Peter Cartwright, edited by W. S. Hooper; Cicinnati: Hitchcock and Walden, n.d., pg. 232.

114. The Great Redemption; or, Gospel Light under the labors of Moody and Sankey, pp. 21.

115. Revival Addresses, by R.A. Tottey; Chicago, New York, etc.: Fleming H. Revell Company, n.d., (copyright date 1903), pg. 262.

116. The Soul-Winner. Pg. 21.

117. Moody still Lives, By A. P. Fitt; new York: Fleming H. Revell Company, n.d., pg. 125.

118. Recollections of D. L. Moody and His Work in Britain, 1874-1892, by J.M.; Printed for Private Circulation, 1901, pg. 94.

119. ibid., pg. 134.

120. Torrey and Alexander, by J. Kennedy MacLean; London: S. W. Partridge & co., n.d., pp. 63-64.

121. God Hath Spoken (reports of Conference addresses); Philadelphia: Bible Conference Committee, n.d., (copyright date 1919), pg. 395.

122. Life of Fletcher, by Benson, pg.158.

Printed in the USA
CPSIA information can be obtained
at www.ICGtesting.com
CBHW022326060624
9707CB00008B/135